Written by Jayla
She Thinks She's Sooo Cute!

An Anti-Bully Book
By L.V. Kern

© Girl Talk Publishing 2014. All rights reserved.

A Message From Girl Talk's Executive Staff

President Kiana Nichols

Girls, I hope you know how powerful and resilient you are. These years are just the beginning of challenges you'll face in life. Know that with great judgment, which begins with practicing it now, you will overcome every situation triumphantly. Display empathy like Jayla does. You doing so will encourage others to do the same.

Be an example and never be ashamed to be the voice of reason in difficult situations. These are the building blocks for the foundation of womanhood. Thank you for your love of reading that has helped inspire the mission of Girl Talk Publishing.

I'd also like to thank my mother LaShawn Williams, father Jamad Nichols, grandfather Jay, grandmother Christine, cousin Latifah, and baby sister Kira who have all helped mold me into being the young woman I am today. They have encouraged me to take full advantage of opportunities in my life.

Big thanks to my close friends (Kiyah, Stan, Paris, Stella, and Gia) who have been a support system and outlet when most needed and for that I am grateful. I'd like to especially give thanks to Ralph Burgess who has become a mentor in this industry and who I learn from daily.

Vice President Jasmine Alves

This book is the first step in equipping you with the tools to be successful in the battle against bullying. It is not a battle that you can win on your own, so I encourage you to share the lessons learned, and recruit others to join in the fight.

Through the lessons in the book, our hope is that you will find ways to recognize, accept, and celebrate your own differences, as well as the differences of those around you.

To all of the victims of bullying, I would like to say I am with you, I support you, and I appreciate the difference that you bring to this world. Thank you for being stronger than those who do not yet realize how amazing you are.

To those who are allies, and take a stand against bullying, thank you for standing up for what is right, and being a positive role model for those around you. This book truly would not be possible without any of you.

To my parents; thank you for shaping me into the person that I am today by encouraging me to love myself and teaching me how to always be a leader rather than a follower. It is only through your continuous support that I am able to succeed in the work that I do.

LaVosha (L.V.) Kern is a 23-year-old native of Ethel, Mississippi. She attended Mississippi University for Women as an undergraduate where she acquired her BA in Theatre in 2014.

She Thinks She's Soo Cute is her debut novel and the first book in the Written by Jayla series under Girl Talk Publishing. L.V. Kern is currently attending the Savannah College of Art and Design, to obtain her master's degree Theatre and further her creative career.

This is a book about, love, acceptance, and togetherness through differences. The words of the characters in this book came easily to me thanks to all of my elementary school friends and acquaintances who have always stayed with me in spirit.

Once someone comes into your life, whether they just greet you or give you a smile on a gloomy day, that person has made an impact. So every connection, every interaction with another human being is a building block to our characters and who we become.

Hopefully, with this book, a little piece of every child can be seen. Bullying is never a simple topic. It is always complex and comes in many forms. Therefore, there is no simple answer. No answer besides love, acceptance, and togetherness through differences - what this book is about. Thank you, and I hope you enjoy the book.

- L.V. Kern

For great character education books for boys visit www.coolcalvin.com and preview the only anti-gang children's book in publishing as well as *Cool Calvin's Solutions for the Many Faces of Bullying*.

Table Of Contents

Chapter One: ***Inevitable*** .... Pg. 1
Chapter Two: ***Bandwagon*** .... Pg. 29
Chapter Three: ***Changes*** .... Pg. 59
Chapter Four: ***Secret*** .... Pg. 82
Chapter Five: ***The Party*** .... Pg. 107
Chapter Six: ***Shift*** .... Pg. 127
Chapter Seven: ***Absent*** .... Pg. 145
Chapter Eight: ***Results*** .... Pg. 157

www.girltalkpublishing.com

Written By Jayla
She Thinks She's Sooo Cute!
an Anti-Bully Book
by L.V. Kern

© Girl Talk Publishing 2014
All rights reserved.

ISBN: 978-0-9770005-4-8

Cover Illustration & Design
by Doina Paraschiv

CHAPTER ONE: *INEVITABLE*

I don't think much of school. No respectable child does. So I woke up on the last day of summer vacation with a heavy feeling and a frown.

It was over. No more messing around outside from early morning until dusk, staying up late, eating ice cream and watermelon to keep the summer heat at bay. Soon, I would be weighed down by books, classes, and homework that could never wait until tomorrow.

Dreading the days to come, I rolled over onto my side and closed my eyes tightly. I wanted to put off getting up for just a few more minutes.

"Jayla!"

No such luck.

My mom's voice called from downstairs and I knew there was no use in trying to sleep in. She wouldn't allow it.

My nose twitched as the smell of breakfast wafted into my room. That gave me some energy. I could smell bacon. I threw my covers off. Eggs. My feet went to the floor. Pancakes! Blinking sleep out of my eyes, I made my way to the door of my room and threw it open. I was instantly greeted by the noise of my house.

"No! Give it back!" My little sister Laya was standing in the chair, reaching toward her twin brother Damon, trying to pull a piece of bacon from between his teeth. "That was my piece! I picked it!"

"I think you're going to have to give up on that one," I said as I pulled out my own chair. Damon was already swallowing the piece of bacon that Laya wanted. "Here." I forked up a couple of pieces of bacon and put them onto her plate.

"I wanted *that* piece," Laya said with a pout, scrunching her nose at the two pieces I had just given her as if they were somehow less appetizing.

Laya and Damon were nine years old—two years younger

than me—and they were heading into the third grade. They had the same amount of hair, which was a lot. My father said once that he wanted Damon to cut his hair because it was too much for a boy to have but Damon liked his hair. He said if he had to cut his, Laya should have to cut hers, too. That made Laya begin to wail and cry, so Daddy dropped the subject and he hasn't brought it up since. To maintain Damon's hair, Mom braided it into a ponytail at the back of his head. Laya's hair was styled with many braids with beads at the bottom of each one. You could always hear her coming because those beads would announce her arrival as she ran along.

"Laya, settle down and eat what you have in front of you," my mother said from the stove. "We have a full day ahead of us."

Mom was a small woman. Sometimes I wondered how she handled the three of us, especially on those days when we were all full of excitement and hard to settle, like most of the summer. Mom had warm, brown eyes and pretty hands. Her hands were always something I noticed and admired. I watched them as she expertly went from pan to pan, finishing up the breakfast she was cooking. Her fingers were long and slim and moved with a grace that— I knocked over my glass of juice as I reached for some eggs. "Jayla!" Damon whined.

"Be quiet," I said. "I didn't even get any on you."

Mom threw a quick look over her shoulder to see what had happened and with a gentle smile shook her head when she noticed that it was just me being clumsy again. A small chuckle left her lips as she turned back to her task of making breakfast. "Has Daddy already left for work, Mom?" I asked, biting into a piece of bacon.

"Yeah. He had to get up *eaarly* this morning," Mom said. She served the rest of the breakfast and sat down at the table as well. "Are we so hungry that we're not going to say grace?" she asked, looking around at the three of us as we tore into our breakfast.

"Oops..." Laya said, dropping her fork immediately. Damon dropped his fork as well.

"Sorry, Mom," I said. I put my fork down and linked

hands with my brother and sister. As we said grace, I thought about my father and how close to heaven he actually got whenever he was working. He was an airplane pilot. He was gone a lot and I missed him. But his job was very important, so I managed to hold in my disappointment whenever he had to miss having a meal with us or a family night.

My father always explained to me that although he always wanted to be with us, he had the responsibility of bringing other people to their loved ones as well. I understood and admired that. Flying in the sky was the coolest thing I could think of. I had yet to get on an airplane because Mom wouldn't allow it but I was waiting impatiently for the day when I would be able to fly into the clouds with him.

When grace was over and we all opened our eyes, curiosity got the best of me.

"So what are we all doing today?" I asked my mom. "You didn't say anything about it yesterday."

"That's 'cause I wanted it to be a surprise," Mom said with a secret smile.

A surprise! I loved surprises! The dreariness of the day was starting to wear off for me. Instead of not looking forward to tomorrow, I could look forward to the rest of the day. Since it was my last day of freedom, I needed to enjoy it to the fullest.

We all finished our breakfast in due time thanks to Mom's promise of something exciting to come. Then we all got dressed and headed out. The day was hot and humid and the sun was high in the sky. It made it hard to believe that fall was about to approach. A dog was growling at another dog in the street and it made Laya and Damon scared. "Shoo!" I said, stomping one of my feet. I wanted to make them leave but one of them turned my way and barked at me instead. I jumped back into my mother's waiting arm.

"Shh! Jayla, be careful," Mom warned. She led us off down the street, away from the dogs. "Sometimes it's better to just leave bitterness alone."

It was when we were making our way down the street that I saw her for the first time. The new girl. She was pretty and I saw her through the window of a moving truck. She looked sad. I think our eyes met for a moment but it may have just been a glare on the glass. I didn't know then who this girl was or how she would change me. How she would change everyone. I turned away as the truck came to a stop in front of the apartment building right across from us.

"Looks like we're getting new neighbors," my mother said, continuing to lead us to our surprise destination. "I hope they're nice people."

* * * * *

Mom took us to the mall. It was huge and it always amazed us whenever we went inside. Laya's mouth hung open as she clung to Mom's hand.

"I want each of you to get *one* thing that will help you through this school year," Mom said, looking down at us. "Whatever you think that might be."

"But we already went school shopping," I said.

"It doesn't have to be school-related," she said. "Just

one thing that you think will help get you through the year, whatever that may be." I looked up at my mother, confused. I didn't quite know what she meant with an explanation like that. "Go on," Mom said. "I'll take the twins with me. I think you're old enough to navigate this place on your own. You have your cell phone in your pocket, right?"

I nodded. I still wasn't sure what Mom wanted me to buy but I figured I would just walk around until I thought of something.

"Jayla!"

I spotted some friends of mine from school and a grin spread across my face. Looking up at Mom for permission, I ran off to them when she gave me a nod.

"What are you guys doing here?" I asked with a smile.

Gathered around me were Trey, Maya, and Marcus. They would be entering into the sixth grade with me.

"Just lookin' around, Baby Girl," Trey said. He came forward and threw his arm around my shoulder. Wrinkling my nose to show my dissatisfaction, I swiped his arm away.

Trey Wildes was too touchy-feely sometimes. He was also a genius—or at least he thought he was. I liked to think of him as a smart aleck, instead.

Trey was tall, dark, and—I hated to admit it—handsome. With a stylishly shaved head, he was well-toned for a pre-teen and he knew it. Already 5 feet 9 inches, he had an air about him that said "I am the best." So it was easy for everyone else to just assume he was, too. Instinctively, he knew how to draw people to his side with a charming personality and a polite word. He had already fooled half the teachers in the school by the time he was in the second grade. And the whole student body was practically his cattle.

I knew differently, though. The only thing he excelled in was Physical Education and since when was that a class that mattered? I also knew he had a sense of humor that could be offensive sometimes and that really grated my nerves. A person's feelings didn't matter to Trey, though. He didn't have time for it. There was only one thing that Trey focused on one hundred percent. And that was basketball.

His plan was to enter into junior varsity the minute he stepped into junior high and become a basketball star like his older brother. He would then get a basketball scholarship that would carry him all the way through college, where he would be recruited and eventually join the NBA. I had to admit that those were all very fine goals but ….

I looked over to see Trey grab a beanie baby from a display case and juggle it around until it dropped to the floor, causing him to laugh, and leave it there for one of the store clerks to pick up. He had to learn basic manners before anything else!

"Whose class are you guys going to be in?" Maya asked.

Maya Summers was a pretty girl with big, dark eyes and thick eyelashes. Her hair was a thick mane that fell past her shoulder blades. She always bragged that her good genes came from her Mexican heritage. Being tough and outspoken, she usually ended up being the conversation-starter among friends.

"Mrs. Newman," I replied back happily. "I'm so excited." Mrs. Newman was everyone's favorite sixth grade teacher. Ever since being younger elementary school brats, my classmates and I had heard about how fun being in Mrs. Newman's class was. I wasn't sure what that meant exactly since I had never taken her class before but since everyone seemed to think so, it must be true.

"I have her too," Marcus responded.

"Me too," Maya affirmed.

Trey made an annoyed sound through his teeth. "Man," he said. "I'm the only one who has Coach Devins then."

"I thought you liked Coach Devins," Marcus said, walking along beside Trey. He pushed his large, square-rimmed glasses up on his nose. Marcus liked to look like a hipster. When Whitney, my best friend, had asked Marcus why he didn't trade his large glasses in for a pair a little more stylish, Marcus said it was a statement, then went into a rant about how people, black people especially, shouldn't try to fit into what the world defined as social norms. I giggled as I thought back on it. Marcus was weird like that. He was a wannabe political activist at the age of eleven.

"I do," Trey said, replying back to Marcus. "I like him in the *gym*, but as a teacher? Man ... He's gonna be tough."

My mind flashed back to the moving van I had seen arriving in front of my apartment building. "There's a new girl on my street," I offered. "But I don't know if she'll be coming to Clemont."

"I hope not." Maya quipped.

"Why don't you want any new students?" I asked.

She shrugged. "It's fine as long as she's a loner," Maya explained further. "But if she turns out to be popular, that'll put me even further down on the cool list. And that's not good since we're so close to entering junior high. Usually, wherever you're at socially in junior high is where you're gonna stay. I don't wanna be a loser all through my high school years."

"Tch. You're not a loser *now*!" I scoffed. "You're the athletic diva! No one can beat you in track. I bet if you played basketball, you'd even give Trey a run for his money."

"Nah, don't go that far!" Trey said. "Baby girl ain't got nothin' on me."

My lips curled. That was another thing I couldn't stand. He called all the girls "baby girl."

"Why you call us all that?" I asked, feeling irritated and never having been one to keep my curiosity to myself.

"Call you all what?" Trey wondered lazily.

"Baby girl. It's not like you grown." A shrug of annoyance ran across my shoulders.

"Psh. Haha." Trey gave me a lazy grin and pinched my cheek softly. His hand felt rough—probably from dribbling a basketball so much. I swiped a hand across my cheek where he had touched me, trying to erase the contact. "I just like to call y'all that 'cause you my baby girls! Why? You got a problem with it?"

"Yeah! I'm not *your* anything and it doesn't sound good coming from your mouth."

Trey just gave me another lazy smile that showed his perfectly white teeth. I scowled further, taking note of another maddening aspect of his personality. Nothing phased him, as if he was on the basketball court. Steady and calm was his constant demeanor; nothing and no one was going to change that. "That's what I like about you, Jayla. You know how to call me out." He pinched my cheek again (knowing that I hated it) and I jerked away. "But you can stand to take things a little less serious. Maya doesn't mind when I call her 'baby girl.' Do you Maya?"

Maya shrugged. "Not really," she answered.

I threw her a glare that said girls needed to stick together but she just shrugged her shoulders again. I shook my head, wishing Whitney were there. She would have had my back.

"Do you really not think I'm a loser?" Maya asked, still stuck on her social status.

"I don't," I responded. "And neither does anybody else. Everybody likes you 'cause you make it so that nobody can look down on us girls when it comes to track and field."

I could see that my compliments were lifting Maya's morale so that made me happy. But suddenly the smile that was beginning to lift her lips started to fall again. She had thought of something that made her unhappy. "What is it?" I asked.

"Not *everybody* likes me," Maya concluded. "I heard Shana telling people that I was manly."

Shana was another girl in our class. Everyone admired her because she was pretty and owned a lot of neat name brand things and the latest products. *I bet she will have the new Girl Talk bag.* I thought to myself. If anyone was asked about the most popular person in our grade, everyone would have said it was her.

"You can't listen to what Shana says," I said. "She's just jealous because she's flunking gym. How anyone can flunk gym, I don't know."

"She's too busy putting her fellow sisters and brothers down," Marcus spoke up. "If she cared more about her Physical Education grade than whether or not she was gonna mess up her latest manicure, she would do just fine. See? That's why we as fellow peers need to …."

I rolled my eyes because I could tell that Marcus was about to go into a long speech that no one really cared to listen to but himself. "That's enough Marcus," I said. "We get what you're saying."

"I have to care about what she says," Maya continued, staying on the popularity topic and not getting distracted. "Everyone looks to her and follows what she says. If *she* thinks I'm manly then everyone will think I'm manly." Maya threw a longing look my way. "I wish I had it as good as you. You're the one that everybody likes."

Surprised at this news, I laughed. "Yeah, right," I said. "'Cause I'm such a cool person. I come to school wearing mismatched socks every day!" I raised the legs of my jeans just to prove my point. As I had said, one foot was covered in a white sock while the next one was covered in bright lime green.

"Why?" Marcus asked.

"That's not strange or anything, baby girl," Trey threw his hand over my shoulders again. "You're just establishing your swag, that's all." I swiped his arm away again and gave him a scowl.

"It's good luck," I explained to Marcus.

"Whatever," Marcus said with a shrug. "So why are you

here? Are you here just to hang out? Like us?"

"Nah," I said with a shake of my head. "My mom just told me to buy one thing that would help me through the school year. I'm looking around and wondering what I should get."

"You should get a video game," Trey said. "Nothing helps me more than relaxin' with a new PlayStation 3 game."

"I would instead ask your mom why she thinks all value should be placed in material possessions," Marcus supplied. "It might be a test. You should come back with nothing and tell your mom that the only thing that can truly get you through the tough trials of school is love, family, and ...."

"Just get a new outfit," Maya said, interrupting Marcus. "Do you know what you're going to be wearing tomorrow?"

"I do," I said with a smile, ignoring Marcus's offended expression. "I already have all of my back-to-school clothes so I think it would be wastes to have my mom spend money on that again."

"Well, I *did* hear that Mrs. Newman is gonna have y'all writin' in diaries and stuff," Trey said, uncaring. "That's one of the good things about Coach's class. He's not gonna be havin' us do lame stuff like that. Maybe you should get another notebook."

"Is that true?" I turned to Maya and Marcus to ask. Marcus shrugged but Maya nodded.

"I heard that as well," she said. "I already got a 'Hello Kitty' notebook to start writing in." Maya's face lit up with an idea. "You wanna go over to the notebooks and look?"

We wound up in the aisle with the notebooks and somehow Maya had gotten back on the subject of popularity. It seemed to be something she was very worried about since this was her last step before junior high. "Jaimie's the smart one," Maya said, ticking off her fingers as she went through the people in their class. "Whitney's the class clown. Shana's the popular one. Trey, you're the jock. Marcus, you're the hipster. Jayla, you're the girl next door." Maya's face collapsed into uncertainty. "What am I?"

"You're the athletic one!" I pressed, my eyes traveling over notebooks. "I already told you that."

"No one cares about athletics. Not unless you're a boy," Maya said with a pout. "Unless..." her face lit up. "Maybe I should go out for junior varsity cheerleading. That's more popular than track and field!"

I gave Maya an unamused stare. "Do you even like cheerleading?" I asked. "I've only ever heard you gush about track and field."

"That's before I realized I needed to save my reputation!" Marcus and Trey were no longer paying attention. They had begun to clash Nerf swords above and around Maya and me. I just rolled my eyes and continued to look for a notebook. Maybe it was a good idea to get one. I had only gotten one notebook for each separate subject. If we were going to be writing diary entries, I would need something for that. I moved on from the more plain-looking notebooks to head toward the more fancy looking journals and diaries with dated pages.

"Stop it, guys!" I heard Maya saying behind me to Marcus and Trey. "Help me think of something that will keep my life from being ruined forever!"

"Oh, that's easy, baby girl!" I heard Trey saying as my eyes found a diary that interested me. It had a pink, cloth cover with a picture of a pen that had words flowing from it. The words read, 'Written by _____' in white lettering. The blank space was obviously meant for the owner to put their name in. I caught sight of a pack of stickers beside the diary and realized that I could form my name with those. It would be cute. I picked up the diary and the stickers.

"It's simple really," Trey's voice continued. "Jayla was saying there might be a new girl, right? Just make her more popular than Shana, stick to the new girl's side, and then watch Shana fall. Easy peasy. You'll have risen through the ranks in no time."

"How am I supposed to make the new girl more popular than Shana?" Maya asked. "I haven't even seen her before.

"That's easy," Trey said. "Do this ...."

Trey was interrupted by Marcus slapping a hand in the middle of his chest to stop him. "Let me take this one," he said to Trey. I walked back over to my friends with the diary I had chosen in my hand. "Have you ever heard of the bandwagon fallacy?" Marcus asked with his arms crossed over his chest. I rolled my eyes. From his stance, I could tell that he was about to wave his know-it-all banner over our heads.

"No," I said to Marcus, trying to keep his ego from growing by the second. "We don't know what that is, Marcus. Why don't you tell us?" I turned to Maya and mumbled. "I'm sure he was gonna tell us anyway."

"Bandwagon fallacy!" Marcus announced. "Also known as 'Appeal to Popularity.' It is the term that basically means ... 'If many believe it is so, it is so.' Bandwagon fallacy is the creator of religions, status quos, hierarchy, GOVERNMENT! It's ...."

"Alright already!" Maya interrupted. "How will that help *me*?!"

Marcus cleared his throat, hating to be knocked off of his soap box just when he was getting started. "All you gotta do is gush about how great the new girl is and if you can get enough people to agree with you, boom! She's in."

Maya thought for a moment. "So you're saying ... that if I were to, say, talk about how great the new girl's hair is—even though it may be a mess—as long as I'm convincing, I can get people to agree with me and then things will go from there."

"Exactly," Marcus said, still slightly deflated from not being able to perform his initial speech. "Then, if enough people became vocal about how great her hair is, even the people who think her hair is 'a mess,' as you said, they would eventually come around to believing that you were right and they were wrong—that the new girl's hair is, in fact, great because the majority of people are saying it is so, so how could they be wrong? The popularity effect would be inevitable."

Maya beamed at Marcus. "Brilliant!" she gushed.

I, myself, stood slightly in awe. If what Marcus was saying was true, it seemed as if we were being subjected to this "bandwagon fallacy" every day. *How are we supposed to know what's true to us and what's not?* I wondered. "Don't get your hopes up too fast," I said to Maya. "We don't even know if the new girl is coming to Clemont yet." I kind of hoped she wasn't.

"And what does inevitable mean?" I asked Marcus.

"Inevitable," Marcus quoted. "Means 'certain to happen; unavoidable.' As in, 'school is inevitable tomorrow.'"

"Whoa," I responded. "Scary word."

* * * * *

"Mom, have you ever heard of the bandwagon fallacy?" I asked as we made our way, walking back towards the apartments. Damon and Laya were walking in sync on the sidewalk, trying to not step on any cracks because they'd heard about what it could do to mothers' backs. They had each gotten a yoyo to help them through the coming school days. I had been surprised because I thought yoyos had long gone out of style. Damon and Laya said all of their friends had them though so I guess I had been proven wrong. I just grew too old to pay attention. As for my diary, Mom hadn't asked any questions. She had just taken it with a smile and put it on the moving belt in the checkout line.

"Uhh, let's see," Mom said with a yawn, thinking about my question. "The bandwagon fallacy ...." When she took a moment to answer, I thought maybe Marcus had just made it up to sound smart. But Mom continued. "Isn't that when a lot of people think something is true so other people decide it must be true by default?

"So it's real," I said, almost disappointed. I have to admit that I was feeling not quite right about the plan that Trey, Maya, and Marcus had cooked up. But I couldn't really give reasoning to my feeling. "Mom?" I said again.

"Hmm?" she prodded gently. The twins began to skip ahead when we turned the corner and saw our house come into view. Mom let them go. My eyes slid over to the moving van that was still parked near our house. Boxes now littered the sidewalk and more were being carried out by some men. I didn't see the girl again but I saw a pair of pink sneakers peeking at me through the space underneath the van.

"Is it wrong to do something for someone when you're not really doing it for them but for you instead?" I asked.

"Huh?" Mom asked back, not really catching on to what I was asking. "Say again?"

"What if I did something like ... give Laya a PlayStation 3 for Christmas, but I only gave it to her because *I* wanted to play with it?" I asked, trying to make the question as clear as possible.

"And where would you get the money to buy a PlayStation 3?" Mom asked.

"Mom! That's not the point." Frustration edged my voice.

"I know, I know," my mom said, laughing. Getting serious again, she thought about it. "Hmm .... Well, if you got your sister a PlayStation 3 just because you wanted to play with it then it's simple. That's being selfish."

I frowned. That wasn't good.

"Because you weren't even thinking of what your sister really wants," Mom continued. "What if she wanted a GameCube instead?"

My frown turned into one of disbelief. "Why would

anyone want a GameCube over a PlayStation 3?" I asked.

"Jayla, that's not the point," Mom started.

"I know, I know," I laughed. "I was just getting back at ya."

My mother smiled and grabbed my shoulder, pulling me into a warm hug. We stopped when we came to the bottom of the steps leading to our front door. "So I *shouldn't* do something for someone just to help myself then," I tried to clarify.

"It depends," Mom said with a sigh.

"On what?" I asked.

"On what your sister really wants. If she really wanted a PlayStation 3, then there would be no harm in getting her one. If you enjoyed the pleasure of it once in a while, there's nothing wrong with that." Mom was staring at the moving van that promised new neighbors. "I wonder if we should go over and help," she said, mostly to herself.

I was deep in thought. *It depends on what she wants....*

I finally caught glimpse of the girl again. She stepped out from behind the van and looked in our direction. Almond-shaped eyes stared at me from an oval-shaped face. She was pretty. I raised my arm and waved. She waved back. What caught my attention was her expression. It lifted ever so slightly when she waved at me and that's the first time that I saw her smile.

Since they seemed to have moved all of their boxes from the van, Mom decided that she wasn't going to help them. "I'll just bake them a cake and welcome them to the neighborhood later," she said with another yawn. "Come on."

She took the twins and me into the house but I turned to look one more time at the new girl. She was still standing at the corner with a small smile. *She's going to be popular,* I thought at that moment. *It's inevitable.*

Dear Diary:

I hope it's okay that I am writing before we're actually supposed to but this diary is so pretty that I just can't help it. Tomorrow is the first day of school. I'm nervous. What if the new girl really shows up at Clemont tomorrow? I feel like Maya will really go through with the plan of making her popular just so she can prove something to herself and to Shana. I don't know if I should tell her that I think she's being selfish. What if the new girl really doesn't want to be popular?

Everyone wants to be popular, though...right Diary? So I'm just worrying for nothing. This will probably be a good thing. I'm just thinking too much. Besides, the new girl probably won't even come to Clemont. Maybe she'll go to private school. I can only hope. Well. Good night, Diary. I guess I'll be writing again soon. This is my first time writing down my thoughts, so sorry for the weirdness. Good night. Sleep tight. Don't let the bedbugs bite.

– Jayla

CHAPTER TWO: ***BANDWAGON***

Mrs. Newman was a pretty lady. She was tall, had shiny black hair that fell to her shoulders and eyes the color of honey. Everyone said she was a nice woman and I got that feeling as soon as I entered her classroom. She was sitting at her desk, watching us all file in and I smiled brightly at her because she looked just as nervous as all of us. Mrs. Newman smiled back. "Hi, Jayla," she welcomed. I felt warm when she called me by name. We hadn't even introduced ourselves yet. I wondered how she knew my name.

"Hi, Mrs. Newman," I responded before walking to a desk that had an empty seat beside it that hadn't been claimed yet. I had to save a spot for Whitney. She should be coming soon. Whitney and I had been best friends since kindergarten. It was just too bad that Whitney lived so far away, because we didn't get to see each other as much as we wanted to when we were on summer break. So part of my first day of school excitement was knowing that I was getting the chance to spend a whole new year with my best friend.

The classroom was arranged with all the desks in neat rows and smelled like new books, old chalk, and cleanliness. Brand new sneakers squeaked against the linoleum as kids went from desk to desk to talk to each other. "Hi, Jayla," voices welcomed me as they passed by. Some stopped to ask how my summer had been as I responded happily. Mrs. Newman spent the next couple of minutes greeting new students, some, old friends of mine before Maya came in a rush and out of breath.

"It's true," Maya said, running up to me and sliding into the desk behind me.

"What's true?" I asked.

Marcus hurried in and threw his backpack down next to the seat in front of me. "We're getting a new girl," he explained. "We don't know if it's the same new girl that just moved into your neighborhood but it's definitely a new girl."

"How do you know?" I asked with my heart beating

ridiculously fast.

"We talked to Mark," Maya said. "You know he knows everything before everyone else."

I nodded. If Mark said it, it must be true. He was more informed than even Shana and her two friends. And that was saying something.

Just as I thought of her, I watched Shana Dees walk into the room. She was tall, thin, and a straight fashionista for a sixth grader. She sported a bobbed haircut. She always said the haircut added an edge to her that most twelve-year-olds just didn't have. "Hi, Shana," I called from my seat with a smile.

Shana nodded back to me, too cool to speak. Her friends followed behind her.

"She gets on my nerves," Maya hissed softly into my ear. "She thinks she's all that."

The bell was about to ring when Whitney finally walked quickly into the classroom. My face lit up. Whitney was a heavyset girl with a round face, a box-shaped torso, and thick thighs but she was not out of shape. Her active nature developed whatever fat she had into muscle. When she wasn't talking (which she loved to do a lot of) Whitney could be found playing her favorite sport: softball.

Due to her love of sports and wit, I had already decided that Whitney was going to be one of two things when she grew up: either a pro athlete or a comedian. Her mouth was no joke. She was a loud-spoken girl who loved to talk and loved to hear herself talk. Half of the class would stand around at recess simply to be regaled by whatever tale she would choose to spin on that particular day. Whether the story was true or not didn't matter. It was all about the entertainment value. And Whitney had plenty of that.

She was carrying a bag of spicy Doritos and stuffed it into her backpack when she walked into the room. She hid the evidence of having had any snacks by sucking noisily on each finger to get rid of the lingering powder. I smiled at that because Whitney's appetite was one reason why I loved her so much. You would never see Whitney without a snack of some kind in her hands or by her side. I raised my hand to start to wave her to the empty seat but Shana called her name.

"Whitney! Come sit over here!"

I watched in confusion when Whitney gave me an apologetic look, shrugged, and walked over to where Shana and her two friends were seated.

"Whitney just blew you off, girl!" Maya said, tapping my shoulder frantically. I shrugged her off. I wasn't sure why Whitney was sitting away from me, but I decided I'd just ask her about it at break time.

There was one minute until the bell was supposed to ring when the principal stuck his head inside the room asking to see Mrs. Newman. We all knew what it had been about when Mrs. Newman came back a few moments later, leading the girl who I had seen just yesterday into the classroom. The anxious feeling I had since yesterday grew.

"Alright, class," Mrs. Newman said as she stepped forward and laid her hands on the new girl's shoulders. "We have a new student with us today. Her name is Kia Michaels. Say 'hi' to Kia, everyone.

"Hi, Kia," the class recited. A new kind of excitement had entered the atmosphere. A new student. *How she would fit in among the rest of us,* I'm sure was the unconscious thought in everyone's mind. Maya prodded my shoulder again and Marcus glanced back secretively.

"Hi." Kia's voice was half a whisper but I didn't need to hear any more to know that even her voice was pretty.

She can probably sing real good, too, I thought to myself, a small pang of envy stinging my heart. It seemed as if Kia had everything that I didn't—long hair, long fingernails, and a pretty voice to boot. She was slim but slim in a good way. I was slim like a stick, no definition or nothin'. Kia didn't look like a stick.

A sigh escaped my lips and I put my elbow onto the desk, resting my chin in my hand to stare wistfully at the perfect girl in front of me. *She's going to have no problem becoming popular,* I found myself thinking.

"My name is Kia Michaels. I live on Camille Street with my mom. I'm an only child."

"I wish *I* was an only child," Whitney supplied loudly. "My brother is a brat!" Titters and laughter sprouted in the classroom. Mrs. Newman fixed Whitney with a pointed stare and reprimanded her but I noticed that Kia didn't seem to mind. In fact, she seemed to relax.

"Being an only child isn't all it's cracked up to be," Kia responded easily. "It can actually be pretty boring ...."

Kia talked more about who she was, her life at home, and how she was excited to be starting at Clemont Middle School but all I could focus on was just *how good* she was at speaking. She didn't stutter, say things like "and ...um ..." or anything. It became clear that she was both pretty *and* smart. Just what didn't she have?

"What do your parents do?" a girl asked from the back of the room.

"They both work in real estate," Kia said with a shrug. "Pretty normal stuff."

I could tell by the excited whispers that everyone was impressed with the fact that her parents worked "in real estate".

Kia was clearly in.

A few moments later Kia was placed in the seat next to me. My new neighbor.

"Hi," Kia said again in that soft-spoken voice of hers.

"Hey," I responded, returning Kia's timid smile with a lopsided one of my own.

I shifted my eyes away after a couple of seconds. It was always awkward meeting someone new. "Can I sit with you at lunch?" Kia asked from beside me. I turned to look at the new girl, both surprised and impressed and also a little flattered that it was me that she had chosen to get to know first. I would have been completely in awe of her if I would not have seen the flicker of anxiousness that swept across her eyes: She was a nervous first-day kid just like the rest of us.

"Uh," I said, with a full smile. "We all sit with our own class at lunch, but ... yeah. Yeah. You can sit beside Whitney and me."

Tension I didn't know she had left Kia's shoulders as she smiled. "Cool," she said. "I'll see you there." She began to take supplies out of her backpack and only I could see the slight tremors of her hands. To everyone else, she was as cool as a cucumber.

*****

"Turkey and gravy with mashed potatoes and green beans?" My nose crinkled in distaste. Lunchtime had rolled around and I was looking down at a pale slice of roasted turkey covered in gravy that looked like it hadn't been mixed properly. It was thick, lumpy, and dark brown.

"Turkey and gravy! My favorite!" Whitney exclaimed. She took a big bite with no hesitation and sopped her biscuit in the thick gravy before stuffing that too into her mouth, washing down one bite with another. She was sitting in the seat across from Shana, who had her two friends sitting on either side of her, and I had taken the seat right beside Whitney.

"How can you eat this stuff?" I asked. "It looks ... *nasty*!"

"Like you?" Trey stepped over the empty seat on the other side of me and sat down.

"Shut up, Trey!" I scoffed. "What are you even doing over here?" I asked. I looked around for Mrs. Newman. It was against the rules for students to just jump from table to table like this. "You're gonna get us all in trouble."

"Ahh, pshaw!" He waved his hand nonchalantly. "Nobody's gonna see me. I'm like the wind, baby girl."

My lips curled.

"Hey, Kia!" I looked up to see Maya calling for the new girl while she took the seat beside Trey. It looked like Kia had gotten her food and had been standing at the head of the table for a while because she was looking unsure about where to sit. Maya waved Kia over.

Kia glanced my way and at all of the occupied seats around me.

"Oh yeah!" I remembered what I had said to Kia earlier. The girl was waiting to sit near me! "Trey, get up!" I yelled. "Go to your own table! Kia wants to sit down."

"I just sat down! There are seats for baby girl down there!" Trey yelled, pointing down to a couple of empty seats at the end of the table where Mrs. Newman usually sat after she got her food.

"We can't make her sit with the teacher! Move!"

"Tch. Man!" Trey grumbled, standing up. "She thinks she's so cute and can't sit somewhere else," he mumbled as he passed Kia.

I watched as a flush ran up Kia's face.

"I've never seen a black girl's face get red," I said as Kia sat down. "But then again you do have the complexion for it. You're really light-skinned."

Kia's face flushed again.

"I'm sorry," I said. "Did that embarrass you?"

"No," Kia said. "I like my skin color. It's just ... other people seem to have some kind of problem with it sometimes."

"Are you mixed?" Whitney asked from across the table.

"No," Kia said. "I'm just ... this color."

"Ahhh ...." I nodded as if it all made sense.

"You look like you trying to be something you not, though," Whitney said. "With your hair all done up and your nice clothes."

"Whitney!" I reprimanded. "Do you know how stupid you sound? How does having nice hair and nice clothes make it looks like she's trying to be something she's not? You're insulting her and you don't even know her like that."

Whitney's mouth opened and closed for a minute as she looked for something to say and when she couldn't find anything she shrugged. "I was just saying that she look like she trying to be all that."

"Don't pay Whitney any attention," I said, turning back to Kia. "Her mouth runs ahead of her brain sometimes. And don't pay any attention to Trey either. He's the guy who was sitting here earlier. He's just an idiot."

Kia nodded and gave me a grateful smile. "So this is what we're having for lunch, huh?" she asked, looking down at the turkey.

"Yep. I don't like it very much, but you can try it and see

if you like it."

Kia shook her head. "I'm a vegetarian. I'll just eat the potatoes and green beans."

My mouth fell open at the new information. I had never met an actual vegetarian before. I thought only grownups were vegetarians.

"Holdupholdupholdupholdupholdup," Whitney said in quick succession, her voice so loud that it caused other students to look their way and become involved in the situation. "You're a *vegetarian*?!" She said the word as if it was foreign. "Meaning you don't eat meat or nothing?"

Kia nodded, her face flushed once again but she kept her head high. "Right. I only eat fruit and vegetables. And sometimes fish."

"No meat!" Whitney said, clarifying further. Kids around her began to murmur in disbelief.

"No," Kia said. She glanced around at all of the people who were now looking at her. "It's really not as bad as it sounds. I actually *like* vegetables. I've gotten a taste for it."

Kia was holding her own very well but I could tell that she didn't like all of the attention. Her face was completely red now.

"No chicken. Nothing."

"She said 'no,' Whitney! Dang! You're making the girl embarrassed!"

"I'm sorry, but when a black girl say she don't like chicken, it makes me a little suspicious!" Whitney said.

"I like it; I just don't eat it," Kia said, her voice a whisper in the wind. I was the only one that heard her. Everyone else was now too busy trying to make their own cases on the subject.

"Why it gotta be chicken?" Marcus asked. It always made me laugh when he spoke because he was always so animated, but I was too preoccupied with wondering what was happening at the moment to be concerned with him. "It's a stereotypical assumption that all black people ...."

"I'm just saying the girl is weird." Whitney defended.

"She's quiet too. Quiet people are a little strange anyway." Shana spoke. She had just been observing the situation quietly from the side as she picked at her food.

"Look how skinny she is! Of course she don't eat meat!" Maya exclaimed in Kia's defense.

"I think being a vegetarian is pretty cool!" I found myself saying. "It shows strength of character." Kia shot me another grateful smile and I continued on. "What made you decide to be a vegetarian?"

"Well," Kia replied. "My mom just always stressed to me how important it is to be healthy."

"Well, it's apparently working," I said, noticing how everyone had paused in their opinions to listen out of curiosity. "You look *great*! Do you work out too?"

Kia laughed and shook her head. "No. My mom is trying to change that though."

"Really?" Big Angie Thomas who stood beside Whitney asked, leaning forward in interest. "You tellin' me I can just eat leaves and look like you?! What kind of leaves you eatin' girl? I need to get me some! I eat collard greens. Does that work?"

Other people began to get interested as Kia responded.

Kia was practically becoming the focus of the table and in a good way. I was happy to see that her tense smile was beginning to relax. Scanning the table though, I noticed that not everyone was curious to know about the new girl. Shana was sitting with a scowl on her face and running her fork through her gravy. When a drop of gravy spilled over onto her new, white skirt she let out a small, outraged scream. And when no one noticed her distress, tears filled her eyes and she stood quickly from her seat. With hurried steps, she left the other unbothered students and the cafeteria.

"Jayla. Jayla!" Feeling sympathy for Shana, I was about to get up and follow her to what I assumed would be the girls' bathroom, but a voice calling my name caused my attention to focus on Whitney. Unaware that there was one less girl at the table, she pointed to my tray. "You gonna eat that?"

* * * * *

When we got back to the classroom, everyone was

shocked. The desks had been rearranged. Each desk had been partnered with another and each desk had a name on it. I was disappointed when I saw that the desk that had my name on it didn't have a desk with Whitney's name on it right beside it. It was even more odd-feeling when I saw that the desk next to mine was Kia's. She approached it slowly. "Hey," she said softly to me again as we sat down.

I smiled at her before looking around to see who Whitney was partnered with. My lip stuck out in a pout when I saw that she was sitting down beside a bitter looking Shana.

"What's with the desks?" a boy from the back of the room asked.

Mrs. Newman waited until we were all seated before she told us what was going on. "I have split the desks up like this," she said, "because we're going to do something special this year. While social studies, reading, and math are very important, I believe that some of the best and most important lessons can be learned from each other. Look at the person next to you." Kia and I looked at each other curiously. "This person is going to be your partner for the rest of the year."

"The rest of the year?" voices piped up. That was like an eternity for us.

"Partner for what?" Maya asked. She was paired with Marcus.

"The two of you are going to work together on a project that you will end up presenting at the end of this year," Mrs. Newman explained. "The project can be based on something you learned in class or it can be something you learned as a team, in life or whatever. Have fun with it. I will tell you right now, the only way you can fail this project is if you don't do it."

Everyone looked around curiously. They had never had such a weird project to do.

"I'm sure you've all heard that I assign diary entries," Mrs. Newman said. The class nodded. "Well, it's true that I encourage you to write in diaries but I don't check them. They would be, however, a great starting point for this project. You'd be surprised how much you can learn just from writing your thoughts down on a blank page."

"So you're not checkin' the diaries for grades?" One of Shana's friend asked from her spot in the corner of the room.

"No," Mrs. Newman said with a smile.

"Shoot .... Then, I ain't writin' nothin'," the girl mumbled, stowing her diary in the bottom of her bag where it would be doomed to spend the rest of its days, apparently. My eyes went to Mrs. Newman to see if she had heard what the girl had said. But if she did, she just ignored it.

"If you have any questions about the project, which I'm sure you will," Mrs. Newman said, "feel free to come to me at any time to talk to me about it."

Mrs. Newman finished talking about the project and began to get into her math lesson. I hated math. I zoned out for at least twenty minutes before I felt a note being pushed into my hand. I looked over to Marcus—he was the one passing it to me. Marcus pointed behind him to Shana. She nodded. So it had come from her. I noticed Maya gazing at me curiously. Apparently, the note had passed her by. I opened it to see what it said.

"I'm having a party," the note read. "These are the people who are invited." A list of sixth graders' names from our class and the other were on there. I noticed that neither Maya's nor Kia's were. "Put a check mark if you're gonna come."

I put a check mark but I knew I'd have to ask my mom first. If I couldn't go, I'd just explain it to Shana.

* * * * *

"What's your problem with the new girl?" I asked Whitney as we walked home from school that day. "You didn't seem to be into her all that much."

The sun was shining bright on the sidewalk as kids' feet pounded down the asphalt, excited to be free of the stuffy confines of school. A lot of the kids who went to Clemont Middle School lived in the nearby neighborhoods, so most of them didn't bother getting on the bus but instead would just walk or run home to relieve the pent up energy of the day. Plus, a small little convenience store stood on the corner between school and home so the kids would enjoy popping in to get a snack with the money they promised their moms they would save or use on something more important. But hey, after a hard day of hitting the books and trying to keep my eyes open long enough to soak in the teacher's lessons for the day, I thought a snack was pretty darn important. Especially on the days like today when the disappointment from lunch followed me around like a shadow.

I unwrapped the popsicle I bought from the corner store and stuck it into my mouth. The cool and sweet sensation covered my tongue and put me in a better mood. It almost made me feel better about what had happened at school that day, almost. I couldn't shake the feeling that something had changed.

"Who?" Whitney asked, chewing loudly on the chips she had just bought. "Kia?"

"Yeah," I said.

"I don't have a problem with her. She's the one with the problem. She thinks she's so cute."

"No, she doesn't. You and Shana just didn't give her a chance."

"I gave her a chance! I asked her why she was a vegetarian. Then she acted all stuck up!"

"Because you looked like you were judging her!"

"I wasn't judging! I was curious. Look how skinny she is! Why is she a vegetarian? It's not like she needs to lose any more weight! Shoot. You think she's anorexic?" Whitney chewed louder on her chips with curiosity etched across her face.

I rolled my eyes and scoffed as if I was about to try to explain rocket science to a small child of three. "Being a vegetarian isn't always about losing weight. It's about being healthy."

"Eating meat is healthy!" Whitney said, stopping to plant her hands on her hips because, of course, that would make her point more sound. "It has protein! That's what my daddy says all the time."

"Yeah, but it's a different *kind* of healthy," I responded.

"Besides, fish has protein, too, and she said she eats that sometimes."

"Mmm," Whitney said with a shrug, placing a few more chips into her mouth. "Whatever. I just thought she was weird and trying to act like something she wasn't. Did you see the way she was dressed? Them clothes she was wearing was real snooty! Did you see that? It's like, dang girl! You comin' to Clemont Middle School, not the BET Awards. You ain't gotta be dressing up like that! It's like she's trying to show off or something."

"She was probably just nervous," I reasoned.

Whitney shrugged again but I could see that I hadn't gotten my point across. Whitney looked like she was getting ready to argue with me from one end of the street to the other. Jutted lips and hands planted on hips all the way. And I was right.

"Why you sweatin' the new girl anyway?" Whitney asked. "You actin' like you thirsty to be her new best friend or somethin'!"

I folded my arms across my chest. "I could say the same about you," I said. "Why'd you blow me off today to go sit with Shana? We *always* sit together on the first day of class!"

Whitney sighed. "Girl! You know I couldn't let that chance pass. Shana is the most popular girl in our class! And she thinks I'm funny, so .... We started hangin' around a little over the summer."

A seed of betrayal bloomed in my stomach. "You didn't tell me that," I said, hurt.

"Didn't really get the chance to," Whitney said. A thought came to her, lighting up her face. "Oh, hey. You ready for the party Saturday night?"

I shrugged, still feeling a little hurt. "I don't know if I'm gonna go," I said. "I was thinkin' about workin' on that project thing with Kia. Seems like she's gonna be pretty popular herself these days, you know?"

Whitney shook her head. "Whatever. I gotta get back to the house and watch my baby brother. I'll see ya later, Jayla."

"See ya," I said. I watched Whitney run off and

immediately felt stupid. What was I afraid of? That Shana was going to come in and steal my best friend? I began my walk home from the store. Yep, I decided. That's exactly what I was afraid of.

I was surprised when I reached my street and Maya jumped out in front of me. She lived nearby, a couple of blocks down.

"Marcus told me that Shana was throwing a party," Maya said. "And she didn't invite me."

"...Yeah ..." I said, not sure what else I could say.

"You going?"

"I thought about it. I don't know," I said. "Maybe not. I gotta ask my mom."

"I have a better idea." Immediately, Maya began to tell me about a plan she had come up with on her way home, one that would establish Kia as a number one popular girl right off the bat. "We have Kia throw a party," Maya was saying. "Same day. Same time. We make it cooler, funner, BETTER than Shana's party so that we can get more people to come.

Shana gets embarrassed and then, eureka! Plan moves forward. She'll realize she's not the hottest thing on the block anymore." Maya waited for my response. "Doesn't that sound fantastic?!" she asked.

"I don't know ..." I said. "What does Kia think about all this?"

"I don't know," Maya said with a careless shrug. "You tell her. You're her neighbor."

My eyes widened. "Why me?!" I asked.

"Duh!!" Maya said, walking away. "People listen to you, Jayla! Now I gotta get back to my house and help my mom get ready for dinner. So make it happen! We can actually be on top!"

I stood motionless after Maya disappeared around the corner. *When did I become a part of this?* I wondered. I jumped when barking sounded a few feet away from me. It was one of the dogs from earlier. "Shoo!" I said. It turned and growled at me. I took that as my cue to leave it alone and enter my house as quickly as I could.

"Jayla!" I heard Mom call as soon as I entered the house.

"Yes, ma'am?" I slid my backpack off my shoulder and dropped it in the hallway as I made my way to where I heard Mom's voice coming from. I knew something must be happening because I also heard the sound of the twins crying coming from there too. I walked in to see them both standing in the kitchen with their hands wiping furiously at their eyes, trying to clear the tears away. "What happened?" I asked my mom.

"Laya had a little accident at school," Mom said. "Now she's afraid of the other kids giving her a hard time."

I looked down to see that Laya was wearing a pair of pants that she hadn't left home in and I could hear from the living room that the washing machine had been recently started.

"You peed in your pants?" I gasped, horrified for my sister. "In the third grade!"

Laya's wailing grew louder and my hand went to my mouth. "Jayla!" Mom snapped. "You're not helping." She was at the stove, mixing together a sweet dessert. "I'm trying to make Laya's favorite cake to make her feel better but if you could calm them down in the meantime, I would be grateful."

I walked forward and got down on one knee so that I could be at Laya's level. Damon hiccupped as his crying began to take a toll on him. "Why are *you* crying?" I asked.

"'Cause, 'cause Laya's crying," he hiccupped.

I shook my head. "Laya?" I said gently, focusing on her instead. "You wanna go to the amusement park? Mom will take you to the amusement park if you quit cryin'."

"What amusement park?" Laya sniffled.

"Don't you even tell her that lie," Mom said from the stove. "Nice try, though."

I clicked my tongue against my teeth. "I'll get you to take us there eventually," I said.

"Good luck," Mom teased.

I continued to try to get Laya to calm down to no avail. "Why are you crying?" I finally whined, feeling at a loss for what to do. "Is it because you're afraid the kids will laugh at you when you go back to school?"

Laya nodded. "I'm embarrassed," she sniffled.

I smiled at my cute little sister. "Don't worry about the other kids laughing at you," I said. "The good thing about third graders is that they have a very short memory. Maybe you can have Mom bake you some cookies and then take those to class tomorrow. The kids will be so excited about having cookies that they won't even think about your accident." I turned to Mom to see how that sounded and she nodded with a gentle smile to show that she was on board.

"That sound good to you, Laya?" Mom asked.

Laya sniffled and wiped at her eyes a bit more before nodding. "Yeah," she said softly in a voice weakened by weeping. Watching Laya closely, Damon began to get his tears under control as well.

"Good," Mom said. "Now go play with your brother until your cake gets done." The twins left to do just that. "Thank you," Mom said. "You did a good job."

"You're welcome," I said. "I just wish every problem could be solved with cookies."

Mom chuckled. "Don't we all."

Dear Diary:

It turns out I don't have to write if I don't want to. But I want to. I think Whitney is ditching me for Shana. And I know that's a stupid thing to think after just one day but I have a feeling, a not good feeling. Things are changing. I'm not sure if I like that very much.

Maya told me that I'm the reason that a lot of the kids are looking at Kia in a good light now. She makes it seem like I'm in on this whole thing with her and Marcus. I really didn't mean to be. I stood up for Kia at lunch because it just felt like something that I needed to do. Kia seemed happy, though. Maybe this popularity thing IS something that she wants. I'm supposed to be her partner for the year (whatever that means) but I don't even know anything about her. Maybe I can start getting to know her tomorrow.

One good thing about making Kia popular would be Whitney not wanting to hang out with Shana anymore since she would no longer be such a hot topic. Maybe I should convince Kia to have a party after all...I don't know. I'll think about it some more. Have a happy night, Diary.

–Jayla

CHAPTER THREE: ***CHANGES***

    I walked into the classroom the next day with Kia by my side. We had decided to walk to school together since we lived so close and practically saw each other coming out of the front doors of our houses. When I spotted Whitney sitting among a group of Shana and her friends, chatting before the morning bell rang, I went over to them and Kia followed behind me. I saw Maya looking at me in confusion from the other side of the room but I didn't want to lose my friendship with Whitney over some stupid popularity fight. "Whitney!" I called as I hurried up to the group of askew desks turned inwards towards each other so that the group could talk more easily. Shana was dealing out cards lazily among the group. "Whitney. I tried to call you last night" I said. "I wanted to talk to you about something."

    I didn't get a response. In fact, no one even turned their

head in my direction. After Shana's initial glance, she turned back to her game of cards.

"Do you want to take the bus to the movies after school?" I asked. It was something we sometimes did. "My mother gave me a little extra money for it. Oh, and she also made you a peanut butter and jelly sandwich. I put it in my locker." Still no response. "Hello! What is everybody doing?" I glanced at everyone in the group. They were all stiff and tense. "Hey." I nudged one of the girls who jumped and then immediately slumped over in her seat as if that would make her invisible. I saw two of the girls glance at me out of the corner of their eyes. At that point, it became clear like a bolt of lightning that I was being ignored.

My mouth opened, my hip cocked, and my arms folded as I blinked rapidly in disbelief. This was unheard of! No one ignored me! No one! I had always been a well-liked girl, or so I had thought.

I felt hurt, disrespected, and most of all ... I felt mad! I pushed my way into the empty space left in the center of the group of desks and stood there, my arms folded angrily. I slowly turned and met eyes with everyone in the group. They all shifted their gazes after a second's stare. "Can y'all hear me?" I asked. "Or are you just not speaking?"

Everyone began to look around, wondering what they should do. I imagine no one had expected to be called out so directly. Eventually, they all began to turn and look at Whitney so I did so too. 'Whatever's going on here ... is it all because of Whitney?' I stared at her until she finally raised her head and met my eyes. "This better be The Quiet Game," I said. My eyes flashed angrily but I was shaking inside. If Whitney said that she was ignoring me, it would hurt me to pieces.

Whitney sighed and stood up. "Let's talk outside," she said.

She made her way out of the group of desks and I followed behind her. We passed by a confused-looking Kia.

When Whitney and I made our way out to the hallway, I wasted no time in speaking. "Whitney, what's going on?" I asked. "Why is everybody in there acting like they're blind and deaf?"

Whitney cleared her throat before she spoke.

'Uh-oh, this is official,' I thought. Whitney always cleared her throat when she felt that she was about to say something important.

"First of all," Whitney said. "I just wanna make sure you know that we weren't trying to ignore *you*. You're cool. You know you're my bestie and always will be."

I felt relief at those words.

"BUT!" Whitney said. "It ain't gonna work with Kia."

A crinkle formed between my brows. "What?"

"We're not gonna look at Kia, we're not gonna TALK to Kia, and we're *definitely* not gonna be friends with Kia."

I folded my arms again. It was something I always did when I was about to get defensive. "Why not?" I asked. Things hadn't been this extreme yesterday.

"Shana was just talking to me before you got here," Whitney said. "She said that Kia's a liar," Whitney continued.

I laughed. "Kia? A liar?" Disbelief was clear in my

voice. "What has she ever lied about? She's barely even been here for a day. When would she have found the time to lie about anything? Are you sure Shana just isn't misunderstanding her?"

Whitney folded her own arms across her chest and moved her head from side to side. I knew then that she wasn't going to back off easily. "She said she's sure," Whitney said. "She said Kia lied about her parents being real estate agents and that she's just trying to look cool. And you know Shana's dad own a lotta rental properties in town so I don't see how he could be wrong."

I scoffed. "Just because Shana's dad owns a lotta rental properties doesn't mean anything. Kia and her parents just moved to town. He probably wouldn't even know them yet."

"I'm just telling you what Shana told *me*!" Whitney said. "And unlike you, I'm gonna trust the word of the friend I've known longer."

That stung me. *"I'm* the friend you've known longer," I argued. "Why are you so eager to call Kia a liar?"

"Because she just is!" Whitney said. "And if you keep

hanging out with her, just be prepared to be as much of an outcast as she is."

That stung me even more. I didn't understand why Whitney was being this way to me. "Whitney, why…."

The bell rang, cutting off my question.

"I gotta get to class," Whitney said, walking past me. "You best come too."

I stood dumbfounded at the door. In a matter of hours, I had just been jilted by my friend of seven years. *Oh, it's on*, I thought angrily.

* * * * *

"Kia, have you thought about throwing a welcoming party at your house?" I asked as I sat down. "To get to know everybody?"

Marcus looked at me, offended. He had been interrupted in his rant about how Obama was more than a president but a statement.

"Ooh! That sounds like a great idea!" Maya said, jumping on the chance.

"A party?" Kia said. "I don't know. I'm not very good at parties."

"That's okay," Maya said. "You've got us." She indicated herself and me. "Besides, havin' a party is just all about havin' fun. And everybody knows how to have fun."

It didn't take long to convince Kia to get on board with our idea, our selfish idea. She just said she would ask her mom but Maya and I knew that it was already pretty much decided. We were about to immediately jump into planning but I had to ask Kia something first.

"Kia, do you want to be popular?" I asked.

"Who doesn't want to be popular?" Kia responded back.

I smiled. Let the popularity project commence.

Dear Diary:

I decided to keep records of the entire process because this was something that would most likely go down in the history books. Kia was cute but shy so Maya and I figured that we first needed to change her attitude to that of a loud and crazy house party hostess before we got the party going on Saturday. Because we knew for sure that Shana would have a pool, Guitar Hero, karaoke, and all kinds of things, we needed to step it up a level and to have a great party, the first thing we needed was a great wardrobe.

Step One: Dress the Part.

* * * * *

"Shana was *not* happy when we passed out those invitations," Maya laughed as we pushed through the clothes in the department store in the mall.

"She looked like she was about to spit nails," I agreed.

"Why do we have to have the party on the same day as her?" Kia asked. "We could have our party on a different day."

"I think you're missing the point of this," I told Kia. I held a cute dress up in front of myself and examined myself in a nearby mirror. Not satisfied, I put it back on the rack.

"Yeah," Maya said. "You said you wanted to be popular, right?" she scoffed. "This is how you do it!"

Kia still looked confused. "How does me having a party on the same day as the most popular girl in school going to make *me* more popular? Won't I just become the loser when nobody shows up at my party?"

I walked forward and put my hands firmly on Kia's shoulders. "People *are* going to show up," I said. "*Everybody* is. Trust yourself, girl! Shoot, trust *us*!"

"Man, dang," Maya said from behind me. Kia and I turned to look at her to see what the problem was. "These are perfect," Maya explained, holding a cute pair of white Girl Talk capri pants in the air. "But they're out of my price range."

I gave a groan of sympathy, knowing how she felt.

"... Um ... I can pay for it ..." Kia spoke up gently from the side. We turned to look at her and she held up a one hundred dollar bill. "I told my mom we were going shopping and she gave me this."

My mouth fell open. "Really?" I said, awed. "How much can you spend?"

Kia shrugged. "She just said, 'Don't go crazy.'"

Maya and I turned to look at each other before huge grins stretched across our faces. "Your mom is awesome!" I exclaimed.

We tore through the store, picking up items here and there to try on. I came out of the dressing room afterwards in an outfit that I thought was perfect. It was a blue, long-sleeve top and a long white skirt. I knew that I could afford the shirt but I asked Kia nicely if she could please buy the white skirt for me and I would pay her back soon. She, of course, agreed, because Kia was just a nice girl and she said I didn't have to pay her back at all.

Maya bought two outfits because she couldn't decide on the best one.

"Don't spend all the girl's money!" I yelled at Maya.

"It's okay!" Kia jumped in. "All of those outfits are really pretty."

"See?" Maya said, sending me a victorious smile. "*She* doesn't mind." She tried to run off and get those Girl Talk bags we had seen earlier but I managed to talk some sense into her, telling her Kia didn't have enough money to buy her own outfits *and* a Girl Talk bag.

I sighed and followed Maya and Kia around the store until Kia found an outfit for herself as well. "I like this one," she said, pointing out a blue dress that would fall to her knees.

"I like it too," I agreed. "Maya?"

"Too cute." We all gave each other high fives for the good work we had put in that day. "Shana's not gonna know what hit her," Maya said.

"Why do you two wanna make Shana unpopular so bad?"

Kia asked.

"'Cause she abuses her power," Maya answered. "She's always using and excluding people and making them feel bad and then everybody else just follows her like it's cool—ugh. I could just go on and on ...." Maya answered all of this as she continued to look through outfits on the department store rack, just in case she might see something else that she wanted.

Kia turned to me to see what my answer was. I just shrugged. "I don't really wanna make her *unpopular*," I reasoned. "I just ...." I shrugged again, not really wanting to say it because it made me feel a little petty and unreasonable but my reason swirled in my head. *I just ... want my friend back,* I thought, thinking of Whitney.

"You just want to make her a little *less* popular," Kia chimed in, cutting me some slack.

I laughed. "Yeah," I said. "That's it. Besides, there's enough popularity to go around, don't you think?"

* * * * *

Dear Diary:

Step Two: Defend Against Enemy Forces

Maya was right when she said Shana didn't take our party invitations well. The next morning at school before the bell rang and before Mrs. Newman came in to start the day, Kia, Maya, and I came in to sit at our desks. We should have known something was up just from the way that everyone sat so quietly in the room, facing forward. Kids were never that obedient unless they were doing something wrong.

A few moments passed and then Shana got up from her desk. She stopped directly in front of Kia and stood there for a moment. I watched from beside Kia as Shana lifted her hand. Everyone saw that she was holding Kia's invitation before she slowly ripped it in half and then into fourths, then into eighths. Without her expression changing, she put the pile of what was now trash onto Kia's desk. Shana then glared at a stunned Kia and me before going back to her desk.

I put a reassuring hand on Kia's shoulder, thinking that was going to be it but it wasn't.

One of Shana's follower friends stood up next and repeated the same process. She stood in front of Kia, ripped the invitation into quarters and then put it on the desk. She sat down. Then follower number two came and followed suit. I thought for sure it was over then but my heart clenched in my chest when I saw Whitney stand up. Avoiding my eyes, she stood in front of Kia and ripped the invitation just as the others had then sat the pieces on Kia's desk.

And it still wasn't over.

A slight rustling started in the room and it gradually got bigger. Maya looked around and gaped in indignation.

The entire class was taking out their invitations and either crumpling them or tearing them in half. I looked back to see Shana's mouth lift into a half-smile and I knew she must have somehow gotten everyone to do what she wanted.

I looked over to see Kia looking shell-shocked and teary-eyed. She looked for all the world as if she didn't know what was happening or why it was happening.

The sound of the bell ringing tore through the air and I got my senses about me. I picked up the scraps of paper from Kia's desk and took them to the trash can before Mrs. Newman could come back in. When she came in and began her lesson, I took out my diary and wrote a note.

Dear Kia:

Don't worry. It's not over yet.

I slid the diary over so that Kia could read the words and she smiled, more for my benefit than hers. It was clear that she still hadn't gotten over what had happened yet, but she was telling me that she would be okay.

At lunchtime, Kia and I went to our lockers, putting the books we no longer needed away. People were moving through the hallway but not many. Maya made her way over to us, with Marcus trailing behind. "What are we gonna do about this?" she asked.

"We send an e-mail," I responded immediately. I had been thinking about it during class, jotting down notes in my diary while Mrs. Newman was teaching her lesson. "Telling people what kind of exciting things we're going to be doing at our party. We'll make it sound so juicy, so fun, so spectacular, that nobody will want to pass it up! We'll send the e-mail out to everyone except Shana, Friend One, and Friend Two," (everyone called them that because they followed Shana around like shadows and didn't really speak much). "And..." I heaved a breath, "Whitney. We won't let them know. So when people start ditching their party for ours, it'll be something they won't even see coming."

"What if the party's not as good as we say it's going to be?" Kia asked softly.

I smiled at her. "It will be," I said.

"Do we even know everyone's e-mail addresses, though?" Maya asked.

I shrugged. "E-mail, Twitter, Facebook ...whatever. I'm

sure you can find everyone's contacts in one of those places. As long as it doesn't get out to Shana's group."

"And what if people still don't wanna come?" Maya asked.

I sighed. "You're such a negative Nancy," I said. "If social media isn't enough ..." I sighed again, "we'll get Trey to vouch for us. He's a jock. Everybody respects what he says. He can get people to come to our party."

"What if he's already going to Shana's party?" Marcus asked.

"Trey?" I asked. "He doesn't go to parties. He's too obsessed with basketball."

"Well, he's going to this one," Marcus said. My brows drew downward; I needed Marcus to tell me more. "I already talked to him and he said he's going to Shana's party," the bespectacled boy continued with a shrug. "I don't know."

Letting this news sink in, I folded my arms across my chest. "He'll help us," I finally said after a moment. "He probably just decided to go to Shana's party on a whim. I'll talk to him and get him to come to ours instead. Besides...he's the one who brought up this mess in the first place." With that said, I closed my locker with finality.

Reassured that everything wasn't completely over, Maya left with Marcus following behind her.

"So ...." Kia opened her locker so that she could start getting the books that she would need after the break was over. "How am I supposed to keep everybody entertained at the party?" Kia asked. "We've never really talked about what kind of games we'll be playing and stuff. Are there gonna be games or is it just gonna be music, talking, and dancing and stuff?"

"Don't worry," I said. "I've got it covered." Although I didn't, yet. I hadn't had time to think about the exact events of the party. But I *was* going to have it covered—that I was certain of. "It's gonna be great. Shana has a pool at her house. And you don't have that. So we have *got* to bring it. And we will."

Kia took a book out of her locker, deep in thought. "What makes you so sure?" she asked.

The cover of the book caught my eye. It didn't look like a textbook. It was thick and looked like a grown-up book ... meaning non-fiction and boring. "Because I just am," I answered. "And what book is that? Is there some kind of homework I don't know about?"

Kia looked down at the book she had in her arms and became shocked. She hurriedly threw it back into her locker like it had scalded her and shut the locker door with a bang. Startled, I could only stare. "It, it's nothing," Kia said. "Just a book I have." She looked flustered for a moment before the bell rang and then she looked relieved. "The bell!" she said. "Let's go."

"O-kay..." I said to myself as she walked off. I glanced back at the locker as I passed it. 'What was that about?' I wondered.

* * * * *

"Trey," I called, finding him at his locker later that day right after the last bell ended. I approached him and leaned against the locker beside his, my arms folded across my chest.

"Oh, hey, baby girl!" Trey said, closing his locker and facing me with a smile.

"Don't 'baby girl' me," I said. I heard Mom shut my dad off like that all the time. "What's this I hear about you going to Shana's party?"

Trey shrugged. "It's me ... going to a party..." he said, pretending that he didn't see the big deal. "Why? I shouldn't?"

"Kia is having her party on the same day," I said.

"Oh, yeah ... I forgot about that." He obviously hadn't. I could tell because he was casually avoiding my eyes.

"How could you forget?" I asked. "We just gave you the invitation yesterday."

"Oh, yeah. I forgot about that too." I rolled my eyes at his lame excuse. He only smiled back at me. Knowing that he was waiting for something, I finally just asked him.

"Okay, Trey," I said. "What's going on?"

That was what he wanted. He leaned against his locker, ready to bargain. "I failed my math quiz yesterday."

Two questions came to mind and I voiced both of them. "Is that something to be proud of?" I asked, taking in his cool-as-a-cucumber pose. "And what are y'all doing having a math quiz in the first week of school?"

Trey shrugged. "Don't ask me!" he said. "And, no, I'm not proud of it. My mom said if my math scores don't come up this year, she's gonna take me off the basketball team. But, man, I just suck at math! I can't do it! Baby girl, I need your help."

"With what?" I asked.

Trey shuffled on his feet, embarrassed to speak the next words. "I need you to tutor me."

Well, that was completely unexpected. I let what he had said register and then I laughed. "Pfft! Tutor you?" I said. "Trey, I can't tutor you. I can't stand math myself. I always zone out whenever we go over it in class."

"Yeah, but you still get straight A's!" Trey retorted. "You're a natural. You're just smart, baby girl."

I shook my head, not allowing myself to feel flattered by

his compliments. "I still don't see why I should do it," I said. "I can barely take the hour of math I have to listen to every day in class. I don't wanna spend any more time on it. No." I shook my head, pretty final in my decision.

Then Trey revealed his hand and I knew that this is what he had been planning the whole time. "You want me to come to Kia's party, don't you?" he asked.

Realization settled in my stomach and I knew he had me. "I can't stand you, Trey," I said with a shake of my head. A lopsided grin formed on his face; he had emerged victorious.

* * * * *

Dear Diary:

Some unpleasant things happened today. First, I realized that my friendship with Whitney is really in trouble. We've barely spoken since school started back up. Usually we'd be spending every waking minute of every single day together until one of our moms got tired of the other kid. I don't know what has changed or when or why but something has and even mom has noticed it. She asked me why Whitney hadn't been hanging around lately. I just told her that Whitney had to babysit her brother. I don't know why, exactly, she's chosen to hang out with Shana over me this year. But I miss her. Does she not miss me? And what they did to Kia today was just wrong. Kia didn't even know why they were doing that to her; I could see it in her face. She felt bad. And that made ME feel bad because all of this party stuff was mostly started by Maya and me.

Second, Diary, I think Kia's keeping a secret. She acted really odd about that book in her locker. Why she feels the need to hide a book from me, I don't know. Is it because she's embarrassed that she reads old-fogey informational books? I don't care. I really don't but dang can't she read something age appropriate or something?

Third, Diary. I agreed to tutor Trey. Lord, help me.

It looks like making it through this school year stress free is going to be tough.

CHAPTER FOUR: *SECRET*

The next two days were crazy. The day of the party was moving ever closer and Shana was starting to get more and more vicious. We had managed to send out e-mails detailing what kind of fun we were planning to provide at Kia's party. There were going to be board games, Truth or Dare, a scavenger hunt that offered VERY cool and VERY expensive prizes, and a movie that would be projected on the ceiling while we all laid on the floor. Surprisingly, that last event is what got people most excited. I had gotten excited myself, when Kia had passed on her mother's idea to me. So half of the sixth graders had started thinking seriously about going to Kia's party. This did not make Shana happy.

"Heck, we've already been to Shana's house a million times," I was pleased to hear some kids saying. "We should check out Kia's house."

Right after Shana's invitation stunt, mostly everyone had ignored Kia and anyone who talked to her, me, Marcus, and Maya at lunch. But now people gathered around to hear more about the party that Kia was planning.

"I heard that your parents are rich," one girl who sat across from Kia that day at lunch said. "Are you richer than Shana?"

Kia opened her mouth to speak but Maya spoke instead. "She probably is," Maya said. "Whenever she goes out shopping, her mom gives her a hundred dollar bill to just buy whatever she wants. No problem." Kia's face flushed red. She had only been given a one hundred dollar bill on one occasion.

This didn't sit well with Shana, who had been sitting nearby, so she responded by having her dad print out a list of real estate agents in their location and passing them out the next day at school. "Kia...A Liar?" was printed at the bottom of the list in red bold print.

"Where are your parents' names?" Shana asked Kia loudly in class that day before class started.

I had been expecting Kia to respond back boldly but she had just shrunk into her seat, not defending herself. So I did it for her.

"Your dad probably just doesn't know them because they're new in town," I shot back.

"My dad knows *everybody* in this town," Shana replied back. "And he says the Michaels have barely even come out of their house since moving in so it's very unlikely that they're real estate agents. Tsh. They're probably hermits," Shana finished, causing some of the kids in the class to laugh.

I had wanted to say something back again but Mrs. Newman entered the classroom. I kept my comments to myself.

"Everyone?" Mrs. Newman called, getting our attention after settling at her podium in the front of the class. "We're about to have an exciting event come up. Career Day! And to prepare for Career Day, I'm going to ask everyone to bring their parents to class next week as a Show and Tell so that they can talk about their own, personal careers."

Kia shifted in her seat and I looked over to see her

gripping her desktop tightly. She looked like she was about to faint.

"Kia?" I whispered. "You okay?"

"I-I think I have to go to the bathroom," Kia responded quietly. She got up from her seat without raising her hand and rushed to the bathroom, leaving a confused Mrs. Newman and me behind.

"Looks like someone's not excited about Career Day," Shana quipped, a smug smile on her face.

When Kia returned, she still looked a little out of it. Mrs. Newman welcomed her back and started back in on her lesson.

But that didn't last long. Mrs. Newman stopped short and a collective gasp rang throughout the classroom as Kia tripped on her way back to her seat. She went sprawling wildly and landed with a loud slap onto the linoleum floor of the classroom. There was a moment's pause in which everything was silent and then the laughter started.

The laughter after a fall. It was every student's worst nightmare. Instead of dreaming about going to school in my underwear, I would always dream about falling down in front of everyone while they pointed and laughed. Because not only was it just as traumatizing as being seen half-naked but it was much more likely to happen.

Mrs. Newman stood from behind her desk and ran to Kia's side. "Are you okay?" she asked.

Kia stood and nodded but I could see that she was already trying to fight back tears. And I knew that they weren't tears resulting from any *physical* pain.

"Are you okay?" I asked as Kia walked past me with her head down and slid into her seat.

"Everyone be quiet and get out your books for the next lesson," Mrs. Newman was saying, trying to get everyone to focus on class again. But it was no use. The class was too busy reliving the "comedy show" that had just happened before them. "It's not nice to laugh at someone who falls down," Mrs. Newman said. "What if she had seriously hurt herself? You have to check on a person's well-being first."

"And *then* laugh at them!" a smart-aleck from the back of

the class yelled out. That created a new round of laughter.

My eyes stayed focused on Kia. Tears were now running down her cheeks and falling onto her notebook below, making the pages grey and crinkled where the tears fell. My own eyes almost filled with tears. How could the students, especially the ones that saw her crying, still laugh so heartily at her expense?

* * * * *

Dear Diary:

That day in the classroom when Kia fell, I felt weak. No one in that classroom stepped forward to help Kia up. No one. Not even myself. I can tell myself it was because I was too shocked or it all happened too fast but that's not the complete truth. I knew that if I went forward to help Kia stand up, I would be in the line of fire for those pointing fingers and that laughter. I was afraid. And I'm ashamed. Mrs. Newman is always telling us how we should stand together to face obstacles. We stood together, alright. We stood together in helping to tear someone down instead of trying to pick someone up.

That small event made me realize that we are still capable of unspeakable cruelty. And I am not as strong as I thought I was.

Oh, and another thing diary. Someone tripped Kia. She didn't fall on her own.

* * * * *

"This is starting to become personal," I said to Kia at the end of the school day. We were putting our books away in our lockers before leaving.

"It's been personal to me for a long time," Kia said, her voice breaking. "Today sucked." She smiled for a moment, but it became shaky and fell into a frown. Unshed tears clung desperately to her eyelashes and threatened to fall.

I felt helpless since all I could do was give her a

sympathetic pat on the shoulder.

"Someone tried to put gum in my hair," Kia said, fighting back her tears. "And then someone else tore the pages in my textbook so now I can't even study for the test tomorrow." She flipped through the pages of the textbook she held so that I could see for myself what damage was done.

"You've no idea what you're in for." I turned to see Marcus heading my way with Maya on his heels.

"What are you talking about?" I asked.

"Shana ain't playin'," he announced. "She's going up to everybody practically bribing them to come to her party tomorrow. She said she's gonna be givin' out those new Girl Talk bags as party gifts. Girl Talk bags, Jayla! Shoot. Look, even Maya is tempted to go."

Maya snapped her mouth closed. I stood still in shocked surprise as well. "How are we supposed to compete with that?!" Maya asked, voicing my question aloud. "I mean Girl Talk, really?"

"Ohh .... My stomach hurts," Kia groaned. "Sometimes it

hurts when I get really nervous. Maybe we should just call this whole thing off."

"No!" Maya said. "We can't."

"How am I supposed to compete against Girl Talk stuff?" Kia asked.

Maya sighed as she thought about it. "First..." she said. "Let's go to your house and see what kind of music you have."

Kia doubled over, clutching her stomach. Apparently, the pain had gotten worse. She held her hand up to stop me when I moved forward to check on her. "No. It's ... I'm okay," she said. "I just ... I just gotta ask my mom if it's okay for me to have visitors."

* * * * *

Maya and I followed Kia to her home. Marcus had gone to his own home. When we reached her house, Kia told us to wait outside while she talked to her mom. So we did.

I lazily kicked a pebble on the sidewalk with the toe of

my shoe while I peered through my eyelashes at the other side of the street where my house was. One of the dogs was there again, at the bottom of my steps. It was lying on its side with its tongue hanging out of the side of its mouth and panting.

"What do you think about what happened with Kia today?" I asked Maya.

"What happened?" Maya asked, oblivious.

"You know ... her falling and everything ...."

"Oh, yeah," Maya said with a slight chuckle. "That was pretty funny."

I glanced over at Kia, my brows furrowed. "I don't think it was funny," I said. "She was hurt. And embarrassed."

Maya shrugged. "Well ... I can't help but to laugh. Everyone wants to laugh when they see someone fall."

I toed the pebble on the ground again with a frown. I hated the truth of that statement.

"Okay, guys," Kia said from behind us. "Come on in."

I walked in to see an apartment similar to mine. There was a narrow hallway that led to a master bedroom. The living room lay off to the left of the hallway. You could walk through an open doorway to get there. Further along the hallway, and on the right side, was Kia's bedroom. She opened the door and let us in. "My mom is busy working in her bedroom so we have to be quiet. She says she's sorry that she can't come out and greet you guys." I waved that away, saying it was okay. "And my dad's out at the moment." She closed the bedroom door behind us.

Her room was all green, purple, and white. The walls, the bed covers, the dresser, the TV stand. Everything. I nodded. I liked it.

Maya wasted no time in going over to Kia's laptop—which was on her green desk with white borders—and opening her music collection playlist. "Taylor Swift, Selena Gomez, Ariana Grande- what is this?!" Maya asked. "Kia, where's all the *good* music?!"

I rolled my eyes and sighed before falling down onto Kia's bed to sit. Sometimes Maya could be so tactless.

"That *is* good music," Kia said softly, "...to me."

"You need more black people music," Maya continued. "That's one of the things people keep bothering you about. You don't act black."

"I don't know how to *act* black."

"That's because it's impossible," I said, standing up from the bed. "You can't act black. You can only *act* like *you*. Being black is a natural thing." I placed Kia in front of the large mirror in her room that sat atop her vanity. "See?" Her reflection stared back at us.

"We still gotta add some songs here that won't make everybody fall asleep," Maya said, still focusing on the music collection.

"Just put in a little bit of everything," I reasoned. I turned to Kia. "You can clear out your music folder afterwards."

We spent the rest of the day remixing Kia's music collection then we moved on to Kia herself.

"Are you sure about this?" Kia asked, her eyes large. "I don't know anymore."

It was nearing the end of September, so leaves of

different colors were falling down outside to welcome in the fall, and Halloween decorations were starting to go up on all of the doorways and windows around the block, including the window of my apartment. It was a window that now sat across from us on the other side of the street as I advanced on her with scissors in hand.

I suspected my nervous friend wanted to sit in front of her window because the autumn breeze was calming and it could possibly prove to be a gentle distraction in the face of her impending predicament. But it didn't seem to be helping. Kia looked like the stray cats I always saw around the neighborhood. One wrong move and it looked as if she would spring from her seat and go running, spooked, down the street out front.

"I'm sure," I said, trying to hide the slight tremor of my hands from Kia's sight. "Just keep looking out the window. I'll be done before you know it."

"But ... have you ever done something like this before? Cut someone's hair, I mean." Kia's hands were clenched tightly into fists as they rested in her lap. Maya was watching warily from her seat at the desk.

"No. But my grandma used to work at a salon."

"And you learned some things from her?"

"No .... But it's in my blood. Don't worry." I reached my hand out to begin but Kia flinched away from me as if I held a live insect in my hand.

"I don't know about this."

Maya and I tried to reason with her and make her see that this was our best and only option but "I don't know. I don't know about this," continued to be repeated no matter what was said. Finally Maya sighed and brought out her best persuasive tactic.

"You want the kids to stop calling you out, don't you?" Maya asked from the side. Kia's thick hair was something that Shana had begun to get the kids to focus on when they talked about her.

"Yeah."

"Well, they can't call you out for your hair if you don't

have none!"

Don't judge me for not finding fault with that statement at the time, diary.

"I guess that's true ..." Kia finally said, fingering her strands as if they were already gone and missed. She only did this for a short while though. After a few seconds, Kia's back straightened and she filled herself with will and determination. "Okay," she said. "Let's do it." She covered her face with her hands and waited for the horrible "chik, chik, chik" of the scissors.

I thought about backing out for a second—but only for a second. I figured I had to come through after we had spent so much time talking Kia into it so well. So with a deep breath and a steadied grip, I went in with no hesitation lest I lose my nerve, and I got rid of the object of the kids' scorn. Kia's locks mimicked the falling leaves outside as they floated to the carpeted floor. Neither I *nor* Kia could have informed each other how things were going. We both had our eyes closed. I don't know what Maya was doing. She may have had her eyes closed too.

When I felt that I was done, I stepped back to witness my creation. A hand went to my mouth and a gasp escaped my lips. It looked like a jagged helmet was sitting atop Kia's head.

"JAYLA LASHAUN BROWN!"

The voice of my mother cracked through the house like a whip and my stomach dropped. The next few minutes were chaotic. Apparently, mom had come over with that welcoming cake she had been talking about and Kia's mother had let her in. We hadn't even heard her knock. Mom and Mrs. Michaels tried to console Kia who had descended into tears after she caught a glimpse of herself in the reflection of the vanity mirror. I could only stand in the corner with my head down while our two mothers tried to find a solution. Maya made some excuse and ran out of the house like her feet were on fire. Finally, it was decided that Kia would just be taken to the salon in town so that they could fix all of the damage done by my unskilled hand.

"You apologize to Mrs. Michaels, young lady, and then go right home!" Mom reprimanded. "I ain't through wit' you." I ducked my head, a weak apology falling from my lips, and knew that I was going to hear a scolding that night. "Come on, Kia!" Kia was dragged along behind her mother out the front door, sobbing all the way.

The sun was beginning to set when I saw Mrs. Michaels, Mom, and Kia returning from their trip. I had been skulking around the window in my house all day to see when they would be getting back. Kia was no longer crying but was smiling happily and my mother's scowl was no longer as deep. "Whoa," I whispered, my nose pressed up against the glass of my window. I let the window up to get a better view. Forgetting my initial vow to fade into the shadows whenever my mother got back, I leaned over the window sill and shouted, "Kia, girl, you look like a model!"

Her hair, hanging right below her ears, was shorter now than when she left but they had evened it out and done something to make it sleek, shiny, and hang stylishly. She looked like one of the models we all saw on television.

Kia waved happily at me from the street so the fears I had of her being mad at me for messing up her hair washed away. But my mother was a different story.

"Girl, get back in that house!" Mom yelled from her place in the street; she didn't care who she might wake up. I immediately ducked back into the house. "Go on to your house, Kia," I heard my mother say in a gentler voice as I waited for the front door to open and steeled myself for the punishment I was bound to get.

The punishment had been a little less heavy than I had been expecting. A disappointed look that left my pride stinging more than anything else and a harsh scolding that made me want to tell Mom to wash her mouth out with soap as I would be told if I were to say some of the things that my mother had said. But I knew talking back would result in a worse punishment so I kept my lips shut. It was good that I did too because I needed to conserve my energy for the party the next day. It was almost time.

* * * * *

I woke up the next morning, dreading the day, which is odd because it was Saturday—the first weekend since school started—and I also had a party to go to later. I rolled over. And it was because of this party that I wanted to burrow underneath my covers and stay there. I was a nervous wreck. "Girl Talk ..." I groaned. "How can we compete with Girl Talk?" I began to realize that the party may have the exact opposite effect of what we wanted to happen. Maybe we wouldn't rise in popularity; maybe we would fall.

"Jayla!" Mom's voice called me from downstairs. I didn't want to get up. Then I smelled eggs.

I threw the covers off.

Pancakes.

I put my foot on the floor.

Bacon.

I made my way to the door and downstairs.

Damon and Laya were already at the table. They were fighting over a pancake this time. "I wanted that one!" Laya shrieked as Damon dug a fork into a pancake and scooped it over to his plate. Defiantly, he bit into it. Laya wailed. I sat down, trying to blink the sleep out of my eyes and gave Laya a different pancake.

"I don't want that one; I want his!" Laya shrieked.

"I think it's a little too late for that," I said, watching Damon tear into his pancake. "This one tastes just the same as that one. Trust me."

Laya sniffled and wiped her tears away angrily before beginning to eat.

"Kia's party is today, right?" Mom asked, sitting down at the table across from me. I nodded, my stomach tightening with worry. "Are you excited?" I shrugged.

"Jayla?" Laya's small voice brought my attention to her.

"Hmm?" I asked.

"I gave everybody cookies like you said and nobody's picking on me …."

"Good!" I exclaimed.

"Except Brenda ...."

"Brenda?" I tilted my head, trying to remember who Brenda was. Yes. It was who I was thinking of. "Isn't Brenda your friend?"

"Yeah ..." Laya said with a sad smile. "She's not picking on me to be mean. I think she just thinks it's funny. But I don't think it's funny."

"Then you should tell her how much it's hurting you," I said. "Then she'll stop."

Laya played with her pancakes. "Maybe ...." she said. "But what if she just wants to stop being my friend instead?"

"Then she wasn't your friend in the first place," I responded. A sharp pain struck my heart as I thought of Whitney. Was our seven years of friendship really nothing to her? "But don't worry," I said to Laya, stroking her hair back. "I'm sure Brenda will understand."

"Jayla, you should go over before the party and apologize to Mrs. Michaels again," Mom said, before taking a sip of her orange juice. "Things were so crazy yesterday that I'm not even sure she heard your apology. She seems to be a reasonable woman so just go over and apologize one more time so that there are no hard feelings."

I sighed, not wanting to do it because I didn't particularly like talking to adults; it was too intimidating. But I knew I had to.

"Hey, Mrs. Michaels," I said half an hour later, facing her on her front steps. "Is Kia here?" I thought I'd work my way up to the apology naturally.

"No," Mrs. Michaels said with a gentle smile. "She went with her father to get a few more things for the party."

At least she doesn't seem too angry with me, I thought, relieved. I gave Mrs. Michaels a smile of my own.

"Would you like to come inside for a drink?" Mrs. Michaels asked. I nodded.

She served me sweet tea. I sat at the table in the middle of the room. "I want to apologize about yesterday," I said when Mrs. Michaels sat down with me. "And it's not just because my mom told me to." I thought I needed to make that clear. "I'm really sorry about cutting Kia's hair off."

Mrs. Michaels chuckled. "Apology accepted," she said. "And no worries. Kia loves it. I think she's been wanting to do something about her hair for a while now. What you did just gave her an excuse."

I smiled, glad that Mrs. Michaels was—as Mom had said—a reasonable woman. I took a sip of my sweet tea. *That must come with being a real estate agent,* I thought. As the thought crossed my mind, I became curious. I still didn't know exactly what a real estate agent did. It sounded cool and successful though. "Mrs. Michaels?" I began.

"Yeah, Jayla?" She fixed me with a gracious stare.

"What does a real estate agent do?"

Mrs. Michaels appeared thrown off for a moment, not knowing where the question came from, but she began to answer. "Uhh .... A real estate agent looks at houses and apartments and things, makes sure they're in good condition, and then they try to sell them to people."

"Ohh," I said with a nod. "So they're house salesmen.

Or saleswomen."

"Yes," Mrs. Michaels said with a chuckle.

"Sounds pretty hard," I said. "Do you like doing it?"

That taken aback expression came over Mrs. Michaels face again. "What? Jayla, I'm not a real estate agent."

I had begun to lift my glass of sweet tea up to my lips again but I paused at her statement and sat it back down on the table with a clink. "What?" I asked. I thought back. Kia had definitely said her mom was a real estate agent. There was no way she could have gotten that wrong. "But …."

"Honey, we're home!"

There was a sound of the door closing and then Mr. Michaels and Kia appeared in the doorway to the living room. Mrs. Michaels stood to welcome them. "Welcome back, honey!" My eyes fell on Kia as Mrs. Michaels welcomed her husband back with a hug and a kiss. Kia looked surprised to see me.

"Hey, Jayla," she said. "What are you doing here?"

I could only stand and stare at her. Why would she lie to everybody? Why would she lie to me?

CHAPTER FIVE: ***THE PARTY***

That evening right before the party I walked around the empty house with a box of snack crackers in hand, still reeling over what I had found out at Kia's house and wondering what I could do until my mom got back home from work. She worked as a librarian at the local library down the street. Even though mom had forbade me from spending more than two hours in front of the television or on the computer, I was thinking about having a media marathon while lazing in front of one or both of the electronic devices. The twins had gone over to a friend's house, so I was off the hook for any babysitting duties.

I was pulling out the chair in front of the desk that held my mother's laptop when I heard a knock on the door. I went to the door, curious as to who was on the other side. I knew that

Kia would be obsessing over the party so I didn't suspect that it was her.

"Who is it?" I called, stopping in front of the locked door, my box of snack crackers still held in my hands.

There was a pause and then a muffled voice spoke from the other side. "It's Whitney."

I pushed my ear closer to the door, not sure that I had heard correctly. "Who?"

"Whitney!"

Sure that I had heard right this time, I stuffed my snack crackers into the crook of my arm and opened the door. When I saw that it was really Whitney (and *just* Whitney) on the other side of the door, I felt happy. But there was no way that I was going to let my back-stabbing best friend know that. I crossed my arms, jutted out my hip, and looked away from the traitor on my doorstep. "What do you want?" I asked in a hard tone.

"Can I come in?" Whitney asked.

I shrugged. "I guess," I said, still not looking at Whitney. "I usually don't let backstabbers past the front step but ... given our past relationship ...." I moved aside and let Whitney walk past me into the house. "Why the sudden visit? You get tired of being ratchet?"

Whitney ignored my question and sat on the armchair of the couch once we made it into the living room. "I heard y'all were still gonna have that party," she said.

"Yeah. Kia and I are still gonna have our party," I said, a touch of pride in my voice. "Why shouldn't we? Are you and Shana feelin' nervous 'cause we're gonna have more people over?" I don't know where the confidence was coming from. It wasn't like *we* were giving out Girl Talk stuff. But Whitney didn't need to know that we were feeling nervous and it was gratifying to know that all of the efforts I had made with Kia hadn't been in vain.

Whitney's eyebrows lifted but she didn't say anything. My face became a question when Whitney's despondent tone finally made me really look at her. Whitney was staring absently into space and speaking distantly. As if she had something on her mind, something serious.

I cleared my throat. Curiosity and worry made me want to ask what was wrong but there was also something called pride that wouldn't allow me to open my mouth to show any type of concern or interest in anything Whitney had to say. In a second, I had been abandoned by my friend of seven years and I didn't want to look as weak as to accept her just like that. I should at least get an apology first. "So?" I asked, stepping on my curiosity. "What did you come for?"

Whitney's mouth opened and closed. She seemed to be struggling with wanting to say something. I knew all about Whitney's inability to apologize, but it looked as if that was what she wanted to do. This caused me to fight a smile. Something was maybe turning around for the better today. The success of the party was an unsure thing, Kia had lied to me and was keeping some kind of secret, but it looked like I was about to get my best friend back just in time for the beginning of autumn. As long as Whitney could get a shrug, grunt, and a "we cool?" out of her mouth, I would take that as an apology and never mention our falling out again. But when Whitney finally spoke, it wasn't to issue any kind of apology like I had previously hoped. It was to issue a request. A request that I didn't want to honor.

"What?" I asked, wanting Whitney to repeat the statement in hopes that it would change.

"I don't think you or Kia should throw this party," Whitney repeated.

I sighed. "I can't believe this," I muttered. "I thought you were coming to apologize."

"Jayla, this ain't about my beef with you or Kia."

"Then what is it about?" I asked. "Because it sounds like that's what this is about."

"It's about …."

"It's about what? You being *jealous* of Kia?"

A flash of pain crossed Whitney's face but I was too disappointed and angry to notice it. Whitney had always been self-conscious about her looks so, in anger, I used it to hurt her. "What?" Whitney asked.

"You're jealous of Kia. That's why you've been mean

to her. And why you're helping Shana turn all the other kids against her. You don't like the fact that she's prettier than you."

"Prettier than...." Whitney scoffed, unable to keep going because anger was knotting her throat and tying her tongue. "This has nothing to do with *pretty*."

"Then what's it got to do with?"

Whitney shook her head and stood up, away from the arm of the couch. "Nothing," she said, making her way toward the door. "I'm gonna go. I thought you would actually listen to somethin' I gotta say for once but it's no use."

I ran and blocked Whitney's exit by standing in front of the door. "No," I said. "You can't just leave. You gotta apologize."

"Apologize for what"

'For what?' My thoughts went all over the place in a wild frenzy. *For making our friendship flimsy! For turning away from me in a second! For making seven years seem like nothing!* All of these thoughts came to my mind but I only voiced one. "You tripped Kia!" I accused.

Whitney's face registered shock and then a second's worth of guilt. It was enough to confirm my suspicions.

"So it *was* you." I looked at Whitney as if I was seeing someone new. "How could you, Whitney? To Kia? She wouldn't hurt a fly and you know that! All she wants is to fit in. Do you know how hurt she was? How hurt she *is*?"

"Do you know how hurt *I* am?!" Whitney cried. I was taken aback by her sudden passionate outburst. "You've been going around acting like you attached at the hip with Kia. How are you any different than me? It seem like you and Maya are hurting Kia more than anybody! You standin' here lookin' at me like I'm the bad guy but at least I know when I make a mistake! You go around with your head held high, focused on this cause and that cause and you don't even know when you're hurting people!" Whitney flicked away a tear that had managed to escape her eyelashes. "Get outta my way." Whitney nudged me out of her way with a shoulder and left through the front door.

I waited until I heard Whitney go all the way down the

front steps before I closed the door on the retreating footsteps of my old friend. Frustration fueling my steps, I went to my diary and wrote another entry.

Dear Diary:

Whitney's not my friend anymore. Kia's lying to me. And this party is probably going to suck. Everything is horrible.

-Jayla

* * * * *

I showed up to the party early with my arms folded. "Good. You're here," Kia said with a relieved smile. She looked gorgeous in the purple baby doll dress she had bought for herself and her new hairstyle. "It's only you, me, Maya, and Marcus so far."

I walked through the door and saw Maya and Marcus. They waved to me from the living room doorway when I came in. I was wearing a turquoise long-sleeved t-shirt and the new pants that Kia had bought for me. "I was trying to convince Kia to put on some makeup," Maya said.

"I didn't really want to..." Kia said with a shrug, looking at me.

"Why not?" I asked. "It wouldn't hurt."

"Oh ..." Kia said. "Well, I don't really have any."

"That's a'ight girl," Maya said, digging into her purse. "I have some. I'll just help you with your eyes, lips, and blush 'cause my foundation wouldn't fit your skin tone."

As Maya helped Kia get ready for the party, I paced back and forth. "Do you guys really think people are gonna come?" I asked nervously.

"Yeah," Maya said. "We made this party sound like it was all that and a piece of meat. Well, a piece of broccoli in Kia's case." Kia chuckled.

"And we got the word out pretty well," Marcus said. "Marketing and publicity is everything."

"Yeah, but that'll come back to bite us if it turns out that we're the only ones here tonight. Everyone will know what losers we are." Everyone looked up at me, slightly shocked.

"What?" I asked.

Maya shrugged. "What's up with you? Usually I'm the one to talk all negative like that."

I shrugged. "Maybe I'm just nervous. And Whitney came over today."

Maya gasped. "What did she say?"

"She told me that we should call off the party." I sat down. "I had been hoping that she had come over to apologize."

"Oh, she won't apologize," Maya said. "Why would she? She's sitting up there with the popular people now. She ain't gon' come back down to our level."

"Thanks a lot, Maya," I said sarcastically.

"I'm just tellin' the truth," Maya said with a shrug. "But don't worry. She'll regret her decision to abandon us for Shana after tonight."

I looked around at the living room, empty of dancing

bodies and laughter. Marcus was in the corner examining his glasses. "Will she?" I asked doubtfully.

"She will," Maya said. "You just gotta have faith."

I looked at Marcus again. "Marcus, why are you even a part of this? I would have thought that popularity plays wouldn't be your thing."

"I could say the same of you," Marcus responded. "Anyway," he said with a shrug. "I just want to see how this all turns out. I've always enjoyed a good mutiny."

I rolled my eyes. I would never get over how strange that boy was.

The minute hand on the clock suddenly read seven and all of our eyes went to it. It was time for the party to start. "Now what?" Kia asked.

"We wait," I replied.

We waited.

And waited.

And waited.

I was about to lose hope when suddenly the doorbell rang.

Kia jumped up to answer it and Maya and I stared at each other with crossed fingers. Then a heavenly sound started. Chatter. Lots and lots of chatter. There were voices overlapping. Multiple people were at the door. Kia came in with a big smile on her face and behind her was Trey. He led in the whole basketball team and a lot of other sixth graders. "Where's the music?" he wondered aloud.

I smiled. From the amount of people that had just come in, it seemed that Trey Wildes was a bigger treat than Girl Talk, if that's possible.

* * * * *

The party was going great. Other people came trickling in as time went by. Music was pounding from the speakers, not too loud and not too soft. People were dancing. There were board games going in Kia's bedroom. The snacks were delicious and Kia's mom only came out of her bedroom every once in a while to check on everyone and replenish snacks.

"It's cool that your mom only comes out every once in a while," one of the girls said to Kia. She, Jayla, Maya, and two other girls were standing around in a group talking over the music. "Every time Shana has a party, her mom and dad stay out there the whole time, hovering over our shoulders."

"Yeah," another girl chimed in. "And her dad tries to make corny jokes."

Maya laughed. "How many people do you think went to her party?"

"Not many," the girl said. "A lot of people just went there to collect the Girl Talk bags, then they bounced afterwards."

Maya laughed and my hand went over my mouth. That was horrible! But I couldn't help but to feel a small hitch of giddiness inside. *Take that, Whitney!* I thought. *Now who should call off the party?*

"I bet she's steamin' mad!" Maya said.

"I hope she doesn't make it worse for me at school," Kia said frightfully.

"Don't worry," one of the girls said. "We won't let her. And we'll let everybody else know not to mess with you, too."

"Yeah," the other girl said. "Count on it. The only reason people were messing with you is because Shana was going around sayin' that you think you're better than everybody."

"Tch. *She's* the one who thinks she's better than everybody," Maya claimed. "She doesn't have anything good to say about *anybody*! We should give back to her some of what she gave to Kia."

My mouth opened. "No ..." I said but no one heard me.

"Yeah!" one of the girls said loudly.

"She *does* think she's one step above everybody," the other one agreed.

I couldn't believe how quickly and easily the girls were getting swayed to turn against Shana. She thought they had been pretty close to Shana. They sure talked to her a lot. Maya sent me a secret smile. Things were going her way. Kia looked like she still didn't quite know what was going on.

"Uh ... I'm gonna go get a snack," I said.

In the kitchen, I ran into Mrs. Michaels.

"How are you enjoying the party?" she asked.

"I'm having a great time," I responded, watching her pour my favorite chips – cheddar and sour cream Ruffles – into a glass bowl.

"Good," Mrs. Michaels said. "I was so surprised when Kia came in telling me that she wanted to throw a party. She's never wanted to do this kind of thing before. She tends to be pretty shy. I'm assuming the reason she wanted to throw it is because of you girls." I looked at her with wide eyes. "I'm glad that you two became friends with her. She usually has trouble making friends so quickly."

I smiled. "Well, Kia's really nice. We all like her a lot." I looked at Mrs. Michaels curiously for a moment. It still bothered me that Kia hadn't told me the truth about what she did for a living. "Are you coming to Career Day?" I asked Mrs. Michaels.

"Career Day?" she questioned, lifting her head. "I hadn't

heard of it. Is this something that's happening at school?"

I nodded. "In the coming week. The parents are supposed to come and tell us a little bit about what they do."

"Kia never told me about this," Mrs. Michaels said. "Hmm. What day is this supposed to be on?"

I wondered why Kia had never told her mother about Career Day. "Friday, I think," I said. Wanting to know, I asked. "So what *is* it that you do, Mrs. Michaels?"

Mrs. Michaels opened her mouth to respond.

"Jayla!"

I whipped around in my seat to see Trey calling me from the doorway. He stopped short when he saw that Mrs. Michaels was in there as well. "Oh," he said. "I'm sorry. I just wanted to talk to Jayla. I'll wait."

"No, that's okay," Mrs. Michaels said, picking up the bowl of potato chips that she had just prepared. "I was going to put this out and disappear back into my hole. You kids don't party too hard." She chuckled and left the room.

A puff of irritation left my lips. I felt like I had missed

my chance to know exactly what Kia was hiding. "Thanks a lot, Trey," I said.

"What?" he asked, throwing his hands up in confusion.

I shook my head. "Nothing. What do you want?"

"I just wanted to know when my first tutoring lesson would be," he said, sliding a chair out from the table. "My mom was really excited when she heard that I would be getting tutoring lessons from you. She bought me a brand new pair of shoes just to thank me for stepping up." He held up his foot to show off the new pair of Lebrons he had just received.

I still wasn't too happy about having this extra thing to do on my plate but I was glad that Mrs. Wildes felt like I could help her son. "This coming up Thursday should be okay," I said. "I just gotta ask my mom."

Trey's lips went up into a half-smile and he shrugged. "Cool," he said. "So how you doin'? I came to check on my baby girl. You don't seem to be enjoying the party as much as I thought you would."

The way he referred to me caused a frown to form

on my fac. I answered his question but was surprised to see him showing concern. "I'm doing fine. I'm just ready to go though."

Trey laughed. "No way!" he exclaimed. "This was all your idea. How can you be ready to go already?"

This time it was me who shrugged. "Not my kind o' party I guess."

"Why not?"

"Everybody is acting weird as if they've been on Kia's side since the beginning. Some of the people here were the exact ones callin' Kia names a couple of days ago," I responded honestly. "I feel like I'm in some weird sci-fi world or somethin'."

A chuckle left Trey's lips. "That's 'cause everybody's not as real as you, Jayla."

I sighed. "I wish we could all just go back to playing with crayons and sandboxes. Life was simpler then."

Trey laughed.

"What?" I asked, offended. "Ain't nothing wrong with

crayons and sandboxes," I said with a good-humored smile. "But nah ... seriously. We did this whole thing so Kia could be the new popular girl. With how everybody is jumpin' ship on Shana so quickly, how can we trust that they won't do the same to Kia once she leaves this party? Things might be just the same as they were tomorrow as they were last week. Kia may still be getting picked on. Then we would have done this for nothing."

"That's what your problem is Jayla. You're so hung up on tomorrow or the next day that you miss out on some of the best moments in life. Like right now, at this party, with me." Trey reached forward and grabbed my shoulders, shaking me gently. "You need to loosen up a little."

I wiggled out of his grasp. "I *am* loose. I know how to have fun. I just worry, that's all."

Trey rose from his seat and smiled down at me. "So Thursday," he said, looking into my eyes.

"Thursday," I confirmed.

"I'll see you then," Trey said winking his right eye. That

was an awkward moment. He never winked at me before, not that I care. I'm just sayin.... He's so pompous yet, so cute and I'd die before I'd let him know that.

"See ya. And Jayla?"

"Yeah?"

"You don't have to be worried about people turning on Kia again," Trey said. "Not if you're her spokesperson. People listen to you whether you know it or not."

My brows drew down in confusion and I jerked away to avoid Trey's hand when he went to pinch my cheek. Another chuckle escaped his lips. "See ya, baby girl."

The multiple statements of care from Trey made things even more awkward but in a strange, good way. He turned to go. "Wait!" I said. Trey turned back with a curious face. "Do you really think people listen to me?"

Trey smiled that annoying half-smile once again. "Bye, Jayla." He left without answering my question.

I shrugged off my curiosity and annoyance and went to enjoy the rest of the party.

CHAPTER SIX: *SHIFT*

Dear Diary:

Monday after the party was Kia's day. Our plan had worked. She walked down the hallways with a group of girls behind her wanting to talk to her about the night before, how great she looked, and how she got her hair to be so perfect. Maya was right beside her, gushing the loudest. She was still pushing that bandwagon thing. A bitter Shana had tried to turn kids against Kia again but the plan backfired. During gym, Shana found a big 'L' painted on her gym shirt. People assumed it stood for 'Loser' but no one could be sure. Whether it stood for 'Loser' or not, it made Shana mad. She stomped out of the gym with tears in her eyes. I didn't feel good about it.

Kia didn't either. But others didn't seem to care. The pecking order had changed overnight.

"Girl, are you stupid or what?"

Ambushed by Whitney's question in the middle of the hallway, I stopped short. "Umm. I don't think I am. Why?"

"You shouldn't have thrown that party on Saturday."

The party. I started walking to my class again, not interested in any talk concerning the party. "Yeah, well, we wanted to." A new thought made me stop short again. "And it turned out to be a pretty huge success so I don't see why we *shouldn't* have thrown it. Kia's popular now, Shana's not ... and I guess ... you're just out of luck. Because you *were* only friends with Shana because she was popular, right?"

I knew I hit a nerve when Whitney stumbled and shifted her eyes back and forth before answering. "Who said that? I actually like Shana."

I scoffed. "Yeah, right. The two of you had never even talked before last year."

"That was last year! It doesn't take long to get a new best friend. You should know that. You've gotten closer to Kia in a week."

I shrugged, hurting from what she said about Shana being her new best friend. "Whatever."

"Whatever," Whitney mimicked.

I glared.

She glared.

"Shana's planning something really bad to do to Kia. She's angry about being stood up by everyone at her party," Whitney said.

I put my hands on my hips. "What's she planning?"

"I don't know," Whitney said. "I do know that she's after Kia, though. You threw the party and now it's bad!"

A foreboding feeling settled in my stomach and I finally focused all of my attention on Whitney. The atmosphere seemed more serious than I had previously suspected when Whitney had first approached me. "She's been after Kia from the get-go," I said, not wanting to seem too freaked out. "This is nothing new. But ..." my curiosity made me ask, "what's bad?"

"The rumors that Shana is startin'... girl! She's sayin'...." Whitney didn't finish the sentence. She looked around as if she was afraid that someone would be listening in. The hallway was full of people as students were still rushing to their first class of the morning, but no one was paying attention to us.

"She's sayin' what?" I pressed. Almost involuntarily, I got pulled into the suspense that Whitney was creating by holding her information.

"She's sayin' that Kia is..." Whitney looked around once more, cupped her mouth in her hands, and then whispered. "The daughter of a homeless woman!"

Shock caused my brows to draw downward. "What?" I asked. That's just ridiculous. We all know Jayla's mom lives in a house. We partied there yesterday. So, obviously, her mom's not homeless. She has a *home*."

"Shana says that Mrs. and Mr. Michaels are really Kia's

aunt and uncle. And that she just lives with them 'cause she can't live with her mom."

Feeling anger boil up inside, I scoffed. "That's not true. I've heard Kia call Mrs. Michaels her mom myself." Trying to calm myself down, I blew out a long and calming breath and immediately began to think of how I could fix the problem that had just arose. "How is Shana even claiming that this rumor is at all true?" I asked. "How could she possibly know?"

"She's saying that she's gonna bring proof to school today."

Thinking back to the night before with Mrs. Michaels, I shook my head. "That doesn't make sense. Kia would have told me if that was true."

Whitney shrugged. "I guess she's not as up front with you as you think."

The easy way in which Whitney made that statement settled badly with me. Whitney didn't care at all whether Kia's mother was really homeless or not. She only cared about a juicy rumor. If what she was saying was true, then Kia needed to be comforted, not to be teased. "Kia's mother is not homeless," I said with more conviction than I felt. "You'll see."

"And why are you telling me this?" I continued suspiciously. "You wanted to laugh while you broke the news?"

I thought I saw a hurt expression cross Whitney's face but I couldn't be sure.

"Think what you want," Whitney said. "I was just letting you know."

The morning bell rang, piercing through the quiet of the now semi-empty hallway. Only a few stragglers were left behind and the clang of metal on metal sounded as some lockers closed last minute. Realizing we were both late for class, Whitney and I began to rush to our room. Thoughts of Kia's problem temporarily got pushed to the back of my mind.

For a moment, Whitney and I were both united in the common goal of getting to class before Mrs. Newman began roll call. Running down the hall with our backpacks slapping against our backs was a throwback for us because it used to happen so often when we were still best friends. We would be lost in some silly conversation, the bell would ring, and realizing how late it was we would speed down the hall as fast as we could. Just like now.

Breathing heavily, we made it to the classroom and through the door. Mrs. Newman was still busy writing our morning lesson on the board. A smile spread across our faces. We were home free! We high-fived and took our usual seats. The two desks side by side next to the wall near the door. Everything was right and good for a moment until we heard a sound off to the side that got our attention.

"Psst! Psst!"

Whitney and I looked over to see Shana. She was looking at Whitney with a confused expression and she gestured over to the empty seat next to her. 'Oh yeah.' A rock settled in my stomach when I saw realization form on Whitney's face. An almost guilty expression was thrown in my direction as Whitney got up to sit next to her new best friend. Things had really changed. I sank down in my seat, feeling dejected. I was snapped out of it with a tap on my shoulder and saw a small white note slide past my hand onto my desk.

I opened up the note and read the scrawled words. *'Don't worry. You've still got me.'* I glanced over to see Kia giving me a small smile and I immediately felt better until I felt worse. The rumor about Kia, was it true? I looked over at the girl beside me, wanting to ask her right then and there, but I thought the subject would be better brought up outside of school ... when we could both talk about it. Until then I needed to keep Shana quiet.

I glanced back to see Shana with a smirk on her face. I couldn't let her spread that rumor, false or not.

But there was nothing much I could do besides holding her down and covering her mouth. And I thought doing that would be taking things too far. So I waited and hoped that nothing would happen until I could talk to Kia.

During break, I didn't get that chance because Kia's newfound popularity was making it difficult for me to get her alone.

"Actually my haircut is all due to Jayla," Kia was saying after being complimented on her hair once again. "She thought I needed a change so she cut my hair. Then a stylist just kind of ... styled it for me."

The smiling girls gathered around Kia's locker turned to me. "Can you cut our hair too, Jayla?"

I waved my hands in front of myself in abject rejection. "No," I said, my eyes wide. "You probably don't want me to do that."

"Don't worry," Maya said, from her place by Kia's side. "I can do nails and makeup real good. I'll fix y'all up." The girls turned and began to praise Maya with fervor. Maya basked in the attention. Things had really been going her way since things had turned out well at Kia's party.

At lunch that same day, everyone started in on a harmless game of Truth and Dare. Again, Kia was the center of attention.

"I dare you, Kia," one girl said, "... to eat meat. The whole chicken leg."

Kia's face fell. This game had become a lunchtime

favorite among Mrs. Newman's sixth grade class and this would be the third time Kia was getting this dare. Before, we had assumed this request for Kia had just been meant to torment her some more since it started when people were still teasing her, but now these people were supposed to be on her side. I stopped Kia's hand when she went to reach for the chicken leg. "Come on," I said to the girls at the table. "This has been Kia's dare how many times now? We should think of something more original."

The girls looked around at each other and I thought they were going to think of something new, but one of them shook their heads. "Nah," she said. "I like this one."

I sighed when Kia shook my hand off and continued to go for the chicken leg. She forced a laugh. "I think it's a good one too," she said. "Make me eat meat when I'm a vegetarian." She gave a weak chuckle and then picked up the chicken.

"You don't have to do this if you don't want to," I said.

"I want to," Kia said, before taking a bite with an expression that said she really didn't want to.

It seems like you and Maya are hurting Kia more than anybody! Whitney's words came back to me.

I sighed and sat back in my seat. My eyes met Shana's and she gave me another small smirk. It made me uneasy somewhere deep in the pit of my stomach.

* * * * *

Thursday after school, studying with Trey, I tapped my pencil nervously against the paper of my notebook as I thought over the events of the week. It didn't sit well with me that Shana hadn't tried to start any kind of rumor like what Whitney had been talking about. What was she waiting for? Or had Whitney been lying? But why would she lie? I would be meeting Kia soon so that I could talk to her after my tutoring session with Trey.

Trey and I were sitting at the kitchen table with two glasses of sweet tea out for both of us to drink. Mom had sat them there and restrained the twins to their room, telling them not to bother us. I didn't notice when Trey stopped focusing on his work and starting focusing instead on the tap, tap, tap of my pencil until he finally asked, "What are you doing?"

"Oh, sorry," I said, stopping my tapping. "What problem are you on?"

"Number five," he said.

"Number five?!" I asked, impatiently. "Can't you hurry up?"

Trey looked offended but got back to working on his problems. "I'm sorry that all of us aren't math geniuses," Trey said. "So what's got you so jittery anyway?"

I shrugged. "I just keep thinking about things at school. I feel like Shana's gonna do somethin' big because she's upset that Kia has become more popular than her."

Trey nodded but kept focus on his work. "Ah, that," he said.

"Ah, what?" I asked.

"I know what Shana's planning."

My eyes widened and I suddenly grew more interested in

everything in the room, especially Trey. "What do you mean?" I asked. "What's she planning?" When he only looked up at me with a humoring "tsk" and shook his head, I closed his math textbook so that his attention could stay on me. "Trey, I need to know," I said. "What's she planning? And how do you know about it? Did she tell you?"

"Nah, baby girl," Trey said, shaking his head and moving my hand out of the way. "She didn't tell me. I just read portions of the book. Shana was showing it to people."

My brows furrowed. I had no idea what he was talking about. I felt like I was in a dream that made sense to everyone but me. "What book?" I asked. My mind flashed to Kia hiding a book she had pulled from her locker from me. "What book?" I asked louder, closing his textbook again.

Trey sat back and sighed, finally paying full attention to me. "I can't tell you," he said. "That's Kia's business."

"What's Kia's business?" I asked, not backing down.

Trey chuckled. "I ain't gonna tell you," he said.

"Why not?" I asked, feeling frustrated.

"'Cause it's not my business!"

"Well, what if I tell you I'm not gonna tutor you anymore unless you tell me? Then is it your business?"

"Oh, come on." Trey rubbed his head. "You wouldn't do me like that."

I nodded my head once to show him I meant business. "I would," I warned.

"Oooh!"

I turned in my seat to see Laya standing behind me. She had one hand covering her mouth and she was pointing at me. "I'm gonna tell Mom that you're going back on a promise. She said only liars did that!"

My eyes widened. My siblings ruined everything. "Get out of here, Laya!" I yelled.

Trey was nodding behind me. "Yeah," he encouraged. "Go tell your Mom what a liar Jayla is."

I smacked Trey on the shoulder with the notepad I had in my hand. Laya started crying. Damon joined in with the crying from behind the closed door of his bedroom. Mom had to come out to get them to calm down. Because of the commotion, I wasn't able to get any information out of Trey. He only told me that he knew that Shana was planning to start the rumor spreading on Career Day. I could only watch him leave helplessly after that, since his hour of tutoring was up.

Afterwards, I went to Kia's house. She invited me in with a big smile.

"School has been great!" Kia said, leading me into her bedroom. "People have started being really nice to me! You and Maya were right!"

I settled into Kia's desk chair, waited until she closed the door, and then got right down to it. I needed to know. "Kia?" I started. "Why did you lie to everyone about what your mom does?"

Kia stopped in her tracks, frozen. "Huh?"

"I know your mom isn't a real estate agent," I admitted. "I was talking to her before the party on Saturday. She told me that she wasn't. What does she really do?"

Kia sat down on her bed, a hesitant look on her face.

"Do ... I have to tell you that?" Kia asked aloud.

I tried to fight the hurt feeling that rose in my chest. "Not necessarily..." I said. "... But I thought we were friends. And friends don't hide things from each other."

Kia looked down at her hands, thinking about what she wanted to say. The green and white walls seemed to start pressing in on us.

"Is it something bad?" I asked. "Is she like ... an international spy or something? You can't tell me because it's top secret?"

Kia smiled nervously and shook her head. "No. It's nothing like that ...."

The curiosity inside of me wanted to press her more but at the same time, I didn't want to push. Whatever it was she had to say, it looked like she was having a hard time saying it. "Well ..." I said. "Whatever it is ... I just wanted you to know ... Shana's planning on spreading lies about you tomorrow. About what your parents do."

Kia looked up with fearful eyes. "What's she gonna

say?"

"Whitney told me that she's gonna say that your mom is homeless. And she said that Shana has proof."

It looked for all the world like the bogeyman appeared in front of Kia's eyes and began to bear down on her. She gripped her head with her hands.

"Kia?" I asked. "Are you alright?"

"Tomorrow is Career Day," Kia said.

"Yeah," I said. "I told your mom about it and she said that she'd be there. So I don't think we have to worry too much about Shana. She probably won't do much of anything when all the adults are present."

"What?" Kia asked.

"I said Shana probably won't do anything when all the ...."

"No. You told my...mom about Career Day?"

I nodded. "Yeah. Why?"

Kia collapsed her head into her hands. "Oh no," she said. When I went forward to ask her if she was okay again, she held up her hand, stopping me from reaching her. "Can you go for now?" she asked. "I really kind of feel like being alone."

"Are you okay?" I asked, wondering why she was suddenly shutting me out.

"Ever since I came to Clemont Middle," she said. "I've been having a hard time. I thought things would be better here. When we were first moved in ... and I saw you smile at me from the sidewalk I got a good feeling like everything was gonna be okay. But that wasn't true. I went to school and everyone was singling me out ... picking on me. I thought I lucked out by having you and Maya as friends but ... you two kept pushing me to do things to make myself 'better' so everyone else would like me. I felt like I was being bullied on two ends."

My heart dropped. Is that how she had felt? Had I really been so selfish?

"Kia, I - I didn't know," I stammered.

She nodded. "I know you didn't. And I'm not mad. Really. I'm grateful to have you as a friend. You're the best friend I've ever had, in fact. I just ... right now I really want to be alone."

I nodded and could only leave the house silently, leaving

Kia alone with the secret that she wanted to keep so much and that I wanted to help her hold.

CHAPTER SEVEN: *ABSENT*

Dear Diary:

Whitney was right. Maya and I were hurting our "friend" Kia more than anyone. I would do anything to go back and start our friendship all over again. I know that she says she's not angry about anything but we could have been better friends to her. We could have been REAL friends to her. Being friendly just for the sake of being friendly instead of being friendly to rise in the ranks of popularity. What is popularity anyway? Shana had it and then lost it in a heartbeat with no real friends to stick by her. It's becoming obvious to me that having real friendships has nothing to do with how much popularity a person has and how much popularity a person has also has nothing to do with how many friends they really have.

Today is Career Day. I hope things go well for Kia. I'll be there for her either way.

All of the parents were scheduled to come at 2:00 so that we could get through all of their presentations by the end of the school day. My foot was tapping nervously from the moment I entered the classroom right up until Mrs. Newman called roll call.

"Kia Michaels?" Mrs. Newman's voice cut through the class.

I looked over to the seat next to me. Kia Michaels was not there. The day was overcast and shady. It looked like neither Kia nor I would be going through this day calmly. I looked back at Shana and wondered if Shana would still go through with her plans to spread that rumor.

I didn't have long to wonder. Once Mrs. Newman was seated and before she started the lesson for the day, Shana stood and rose her hand. "Mrs. Newman."

Mrs. Newman looked her way. I held my breath.

"Yes, Shana?"

"I'm sad that Kia isn't here; I was really looking forward to hearing her mother speak. Is it possible that we can hold Career Day on another day?"

Mrs. Newman smiled sadly and shook her head. She was naïve of Shana's double motives in wanting to address this question in front of the whole class. "I'm afraid that's not possible," Mrs. Newman answered. "We've already invited all the parents here. They're busy people so we can't just change the schedule so suddenly like that."

"Oh," Shana looked down with a falsely saddened expression on her face. "Well, I happened to find this book that her *aunt* wrote." I turned to see Shana holding up a book. Just from a glance, I could tell that it was the same book that Kia had hidden from my view when she had opened her locker. "It tells the story of a brilliant young woman who becomes a junkie and then becomes homeless. It's really sad stuff. Oh, but there's a happy ending ... or at least a kind of happy ending ... because it ends with the woman agreeing to get treatment. She needs it—see—so that she can have the option of seeing her daughter. Her daughter, Kia Michaels. Because apparently," Shana raised the book above her head as she made her statement, "the junkie homeless woman in this book who lost all rights to see her daughter is Kia's very own mother!!! And she agreed to let her sister, who likes to write for a hobby, tell her story in a book because she wants other people to feel that it's okay to get treatment."

Everyone in the class looked around at each other, trying to piece together the information they had just heard. My eyes were wide with shock. I had caught every word.

"That's right everybody," Shana continued. "Kia's a liar! She told us her mother was a real estate agent."

"Shana, that's enough," Mrs. Newman said, standing up. She had finally gotten over her own shock.

"And she let us believe that the woman she lived with was her mother when it's not!"

"Shana!" Mrs. Newman snapped.

"She's not the daughter of a successful real estate

agent. She's the daughter of a cracked out, junkie, homeless woman!!!"

"Shana! Detention! Now!"

I clutched at my heart. It hurt. I felt for Kia. I felt for my friend. If this was true ... it was so much more important than what we had been pushing for, a new popularity spot that didn't even really mean anything, especially now.

"Can you believe this?" Maya asked me as we walked out of the classroom for break.

"No," I said. "It's horrible."

"Yeah, it is. I can't believe we spent so much time trying to make the daughter of an addict popular. She'll never be as popular as Shana after this."

I stopped walking in disbelief. *"That's* what you're upset about?" I asked.

"Yeah," Maya said, looking at me with an air of confusion. "What else would I be upset about?"

"If this is true," I said. "Kia is probably hurting. She needs us."

"Yeah, well, I needed *her*," Maya said, not wanting to be reasoned with. "I needed her to be perfect! Now I'll never taste popularity again." Maya stomped off while I just stared at her back in a shocked state.

After the break, everyone was pressing Shana for details. Like the news was something to be discussed and dissected. There was no empathy or concern present, only the greedy desire to know more.

I couldn't even pay attention when the parents came in to discuss their careers. When my mom began to speak, I only wanted to run into her arms and hug her. Tell her how much I loved her and was glad that she was there for me. The bell rang at the end of the day and I went to her.

"Mom," I said. I didn't realize until Mom was looking into my face that I wanted to cry. My voice broke and tears filled my eyes.

"What is it?" Mom asked, bending down to reach my level. She wiped at my tears before they could fall, her gentle and elegant hands soft against my face.

"I think my friend has been going through something," I said. "And I haven't been there for her. I was too focused on myself and what I wanted."

Mom hugged me close and I felt warm. I needed that warmth. "Oh, baby," she said. "It's okay. It's okay." She patted my back. "We can only do the best we can with what we know. I'm sure your friend knows that you'd be there for her if and whenever you could. You're a nice girl, Jayla, and anybody can see that."

I knew my mom was right but I still felt bad. I had only been focused on winning Whitney back as my friend and the dumb play for popularity when Kia had been dealing with real problems. I felt like a terrible friend.

* * * * *

It had begun to rain when school was over and I went over to Kia's house. The rain droplets were fat and heavy. They landed like small stones against my skin and sounded like drums against my rain jacket. I stepped into a puddle before climbing the steps and I pressed Kia's doorbell. There was no answer at first. I pressed it again. Again, nothing. When I pressed it a third time and still didn't get an answer I turned to go. But then the door opened. Mrs. Michaels was standing there.

"Hello, Jayla," she said, her usual warm smile not quite as warm that day. "Kia's in her room. Do you want to see her?"

I could only nod. Mrs. Michaels led me to her room and then left me there. "I think she's waiting for you," she said as parting words.

I faced the door, feeling scared for some reason. The door seemed suddenly thick and wide and when I opened it, it felt heavy.

Kia was on her bed with her knees pulled up to her chest. I entered cautiously. "Kia?"

She didn't look my way but she blinked her acknowledgement. "How bad was it?" She asked. The rain's rhythm pattered outside her window and over our words.

I sat down on the bed beside Kia. "Shana spread the rumor at the beginning of class," I replied honestly. "She said she read a book that your aunt wrote and it's about your mother. She showed everyone the book."

Kia looked defeated. "Is it true?" I had to ask. "What Shana said? What the book is about?"

Kia swallowed deeply and nodded. My heart clenched for her and the room grew so silent you could hear our hearts beating. "Oh, Kia," I said, wishing I could say something that would make it all better but having nothing. "I don't know what to say," I said, again trying to be as honest as I possibly could.

"I feel angry at my mom," Kia said. "I feel like she abandoned me. Even though I know she's just sick. At least, that's what my aunt says. She says my mom can't help it. But that she's trying to get help right now. So when I moved here and everyone thought that Aunt Mya was my mother, I let them believe it. I wanted everybody to believe it because my aunt isn't as shameful as my mother." Kia's face collapsed and a silent sob escaped her lips. "And then I feel like a horrible person because I'm ashamed of my mother." A tear trickled down my own cheek as I watched Kia break down in front of me. She looked at me with a question on her face. "Am I a bad person, Jayla? For feeling that way about my mom?"

I wrapped Kia in a hug. "No," I said. "No, you're not. You're just trying to make sense of things just like she is. It's the illness you're ashamed of, not your mother. Because moms do the best they can for us. And you know that."

Kia laid across the bed resting her head on a pillow as she played with tassels attached to her comforter. She was in deep thought. "I keep thinking about what you said about naturally being black," she said after a while. "Just like we can't change something as permanent and true as the color of our skin, we can't change the people who share our blood. My mom is my mom and she will always be my mom. I either have to accept it or live with all this guilt, anger, and these negative feelings that I've been holding in. It doesn't feel good so I just want to accept it."

I nodded. "Do that then," I encouraged. "Accept it. And you'll be okay because you have people to help get you through. Like your aunt, your uncle, and me."

There was another moment of silence. The pitter patter of the rain outside began to slow until only the stray drops falling from the rooftop to the pavement could be heard.

"How did people at school take it?" Kia finally asked. "Am I a loser again?"

"You were never a loser, Kia," I said. "And you're not now. Because you have me as a friend. It doesn't matter what anyone says when we show up to school on Monday. Because we'll have each other to depend on and that's all that matters. One solid friendship is much better than a thousand fragile ones."

Kia sat up and smiled. "You're so deep," she said.

I chuckled. "Shut up," I said with affection. "I'm trying to comfort you here."

Kia wrapped her arms around me in a tight hug. "I'm

glad you're my neighbor, Jayla Brown."

I hugged her back. "I'm glad you're my friend, Kia Michaels."

"Hey," Kia said, suddenly thinking of something. "Have you given any thought to that project Mrs. Newman was talking about in the first week?"

"Actually, I have," I responded. "I was thinking about it last night. And I think I have an idea."

CHAPTER EIGHT: ***RESULTS***

"Hey, Whitney." It was Monday morning and I approached Whitney at her locker. Trying to pull a book from its place beneath a stack of books, Whitney peered around her locker door. A wary expression crossed her face. She wondered why I was coming up to greet her as if it were a month ago and the last few weeks hadn't happened.

"What's up?" Whitney asked.

"Just wondering what you were doing," I said with a shrug. "Have you been doing well lately?"

Whitney squinted as she looked at me, trying to decide if she was being teased or not. "Nooo ..." Whitney said. "Not exactly. Why?"

I shrugged again. "I was just wondering. I hate that

you're not feeling so well. What's wrong?"

"Uh ...." Whitney looked as if she didn't know what to do. I was talking to her as if we had never stopped being friends. It was weird, I admit.

"Come on!" I urged Whitney. "Give me some details. I'm not your enemy, you know? I just wanted to check in with you after everything."

"No." Whitney tilted her head, still trying to figure out what was going on. "Are you making fun of me?" she asked.

"No!" I said. "I'm really just curious. I wanna make things good between us again."

Whitney blinked and the ghost of a smile touched her lips. "Well ...." Whitney shrugged and closed her locker, giving up on the book that she had been wrestling with. "Uh ... I've just been really down about not talking to you all the time I guess." She faltered in her steps. "And about that ... I've been wanting to tell you that ... well ... you know ... I'm sorry and stuff. I didn't mean to cut you out completely like that. I just wanted to try something new with being popular and all. It just kinda ... got out of hand. I didn't really like what happened on Friday."

I began to walk down the hallway with Whitney. It was odd how our steps immediately began to sync up again as if we were never out of step at all. "It's cool," I said. "Things got kind of crazy for me for a while there too. I was so obsessed with not losing you as a friend that I completely overlooked the fact that I could just talk to you about it."

Whitney laughed. "Yeah," she said. "We've been acting kind of stupid, huh?"

I chuckled and nodded.

"Um ..." Whitney started. "How is Kia?"

"She's okay," I responded. "She'll be okay."

We pushed by students rushing to get to their faraway classrooms before the morning bell rang. "I learned a lot about you this year, though, Whitney," I said teasingly. "I never thought you'd be the kind of person to give in to peer pressure."

"You sayin' I gave in to peer pressure?" Whitney asked. She had a bit of edge in her voice but I knew that she was joking. It really was so easy and simple. I wondered why I hadn't just tried to talk normally to Whitney before. *I just gave in to the dramatics of it all.* And like she just said, I also gave in to peer pressure. I shushed the voice in my head and continued to walk alongside Whitney.

"Hey, Jayla. Sorry about yesterday," a kid from gym class spoke as she passed Whitney and me. Her name was Mika but I didn't know much about the girl. I just knew that she usually hung out with Shana and her friends. She was also good friends with Trey because she played basketball as a hobby. *I wonder why she's apologizing to me,* I wondered momentarily before shaking my head. *It's Kia who needs to be apologized to.*

"Yeah," Whitney said. "I'm sorry about yesterday too. I really didn't know that was gonna happen."

I smiled. "It's all good, girl. I don't even wanna talk about it."

"You were cool though," Whitney said. "I could tell how much you cared about Kia just from how you reacted to the news. It made me realize that Shana had gone a little too far."

"Ahhh. Let's not talk about it," I said again, embarrassment washing over me anew. "Was it really so easy to tell that I was about to break down crying?"

"Girl, you're easier to read than newspaper," Whitney said with a laugh. We then began to fall into an easy conversation that led us all the way to the classroom and to our seats. Mrs. Newman was just writing the bell ringer on the board and I was about to sit down when I heard Kia's voice.

"Hey, Jayla."

My stomach churned with instant nervousness. In bed the night before, I had been going over and over how we would do things today. In the light of day on Monday I was beginning to think that I had been too hasty in my plans.

"Hey, Kia," I said. "Are you ready?" I said the words quickly before I could lose my nerve.

"What are you two talking about?" Whitney asked, curious.

"You'll see," I said, flashing her a small smile.

"Okay," Mrs. Newman said, starting the lesson. "Are we all ready to start the day?"

Battling my nerves, I raised my hand. "Mrs. Newman?"

"Yes, Jayla?"

"Kia and I would like to do the presentation for our project today. We think we're ready."

Mrs. Newman's eyes widened. "The project that's not due until the end of the year? Are you sure?"

I nodded. "We're sure."

Mrs. Newman's face lit up. Her eyes and smile were warm. She seemed excited. "Okay," she said. "Since the project is supposed to come from a completely organic place, I can only trust that you would know yourself when you felt ready to present it. Go ahead."

Kia and I stood before the class. I suppressed the butterflies in my stomach and began our presentation.

"At first, like everyone else, I had no idea what Mrs. Newman wanted when she assigned this project to us. And honestly, since it was due at the end of the year, I filed it away in the back of my mind as something to think about a week from the end of the year." Everyone chuckled. I was relieved to look over to see that Mrs. Newman had chuckled as well. "But Kia and I have been through a lot in these first few weeks. I realized it last week when I was reading through my diary entries. That's when I came up with what I wanted to do the presentation on."

I pulled out my diary and handed it to Kia.

"I want Kia to read my diary aloud. Every entry. This will be her first time seeing it or reading it. But I want her to read it because I've learned a lot about Kia over the past few days. And I'd like for her to learn a lot about me too. After going back and reading the words I wrote days and weeks ago, I was able to clearly see when I was being selfish, happy, angry, forgiving, truthful ... There were no lies in my diary. I guess that's what the beauty of a diary is.

"When Kia first arrived, I was a part of a plan to try to make her into a popular new girl. I didn't become her friend just to become her friend. But after reading these, I hope that she can see exactly what I was feeling, thinking, and hoping in the days that I was with her. And I hope that after reading these, she can know me for who I truly am; so that I really can be the *best* friend possible. And I wanted to share it with all of you so that I could open myself up to being your friend too. Your true friend. Because what I've learned is that popularity is nothing. Friendship is what matters."

After my words, I looked at Kia, letting her know that I was ready for her to start reading. I sat down in the chair beside her at the front of the class as she cracked the book open and began to read. It was the most uncomfortable I had been in a long time. I felt exposed and open and out there as Kia read my words to the class. But I didn't take my eyes off of my classmates until she was done. It was their choice whether they wanted to judge me or laugh with me or cry with me but I was taking them on a journey with me. My journey. And Kia's journey. When Kia finished reading, there was a moment of silence and then the class applauded.

I didn't know if they were applauding because it was

over or because they appreciated what I shared with them or if they were just applauding for the sake of applauding. I don't know if half of them even understood what the point of our presentation was. And I didn't know how Mrs. Newman was going to grade me on it. But I was happy. And I was free to start anew with my friendship with Kia. I really feel that Kia's arrival in my life was a good thing. It was fate. It was inevitable.

And standing there in front of the class, I realized that I *did* have the inner strength of leadership that Trey had been talking about. Maybe I didn't have as many friends as Trey or as many followers as Shana, but I had a voice. And people listened.

* * * * *

Dear Diary:

We all have a voice. Marcus's voice resonates. Trey's voice soothes. Whitney's voice entertains. And Kia's voice is quiet. But her voice never changes. I can't say that things changed for the better all at once, Diary. This is real life and real life doesn't wrap up with a "happily ever after." All the people in the class clapped and applauded but not all understood. Kia didn't become the new "It" girl just because of my short and flawed speech. But she had me and Whitney. And then a few others once the next semester started. It was a slow change but true change rarely ever happens all at once.

There definitely is no miracle cure for bullying or no easy answers on how to handle it. I'm not sure if there ever will be. The only thing we can do is love ourselves and others. If I ever see a girl standing alone, I know now that I will invite her over to sit with me. If I hear a girl whisper, I'm going to lean in so that I can hear her speak. And if I see someone crying, I'm going to do everything I can to make them smile again. That's my vow to you, Diary. And since it's my written word, it's a promise.

This writing thing isn't so bad. Until next time...

~ Jayla

THE END

Made in the USA
Columbia, SC
25 August 2020